Andrew Simon Lamb

The Gospel and the Child

Andrew Simon Lamb

The Gospel and the Child

ISBN/EAN: 9783337285654

Printed in Europe, USA, Canada, Australia, Japan

Cover: Foto ©Lupo / pixelio.de

More available books at **www.hansebooks.com**

THE GOSPEL AND THE CHILD.

BY

ANDREW SIMON LAMB,

SCOTCH ADVOCATE,
OF THE INNER TEMPLE,
BARRISTER-AT-LAW.

'I speak as to wise men; judge ye what I say.'

LONDON:
JAMES NISBET & CO., 21 BERNERS STREET.
1884.

PREFACE.

FOR years the writer has laboured under the sad but settled conviction that much of what passes for Christian upbringing, though fairly enough entitled to the designation of religious, cannot be justly denominated gospel.

Under the name of Christian there seems not unfrequently employed a system of instruction, which so conceals the doctrines of the Cross beneath an ostentatious regard to the professed vindication of the Law, that such training might be well described as legal rather than evangelical. The Gospel is indeed acknowledged and extolled, but it is treated withal rather as a remedy to be explained and accepted by and by, after a fitting period of preparation or probation, than employed and most truly honoured as a present and readily available salvation—for time as for eternity—for childhood as for old age.

If however the reception of the gospel in all its simplicity and fulness, is the *only* mean for introducing into the heart the constraining love of Christ, and it is in the presence of that love as a motive power that we have alone a sure and sufficient guarantee for the just and truly adequate use of life, if that gospel is kept back, on any pretence whatever, it is vain to hope that its place can be supplied by any extraneous or moral coercion, however well systematized or even apparently sanctioned by, or professedly founded on the very law itself.

It is futile to hope that by any other means than the acceptance of the gospel, the human can be brought into that submission to, and acquiescence with, the divine will which is indispensable to the right appreciation and employment of the opportunities and advantages of life.

There seems a widespread tendency, not indeed avowed, but all the same practical (a tendency against which, moreover, the loudest professions of regard for the doctrines of the resuscitated faith of the Reformation, may not unfrequently fail to afford any real or absolute security), to virtually substitute in the upbringing of the young, law for gospel, or rather perhaps to employ, as a temporary expedient for the years of childhood, what might be perhaps not untruly described as an attempted combination of law with gospel, in which the former is allowed to predominate, to the almost practical subversion of the latter.

Consideration of the necessary and natural consequences of the adoption of such a course, not only affords ready and reasonable explanation for much of the general, spiritual and moral, inefficiency of the ordinary religious instruction of the school, but also supplies a very reasonable solution of the so common difficulty suggested by the downright, manifest, and sometimes appalling failures of the children of most religious parents, or of the pupils of strictest and sternest preceptors.

May He Who was so loving and merciful to the writer through a long protracted career of folly, profligacy, and sin, and has now vouchsafed prosperity, blessing, and comfort in the preparation of this volume, employ its unworthy tribute to the absolute indispensability, not only of His purchased pardon, but of His finished righteousness, from one who trusts however feebly in both, for God's glory, through the good of man, especially of the young, as may be in accordance with His holy will. To His name be all the praise.

1 PAPER BUILDINGS, TEMPLE,
    1884.

CONTENTS.

CHAP.		PAGE
I.	BELIEF,	11
II.	UPBRINGING,	24
III.	THE BIBLE,	33
IV.	MEANS,	47
V.	HUMAN NATURE,	57
VI.	THE END OF EXISTENCE,	73
VII.	THE GOSPEL,	84
VIII.	SURROUNDINGS,	106
IX.	APPLICATION,	120
X.	OBJECT AND MOTIVE,	137
XI.	GOSPEL INSTRUCTION,	148
XII.	JUSTIFICATION AND SANCTIFICATION,	174
XIII.	ADVANTAGES,	206
XIV.	GETTING ON,	226
XV.	CONCLUSION,	241

THE GOSPEL AND THE CHILD.

CHAPTER I.

BELIEF.

A BELIEVER in anything is one who in his plans or actions takes its existence into account whenever in his judgment it affects or may possibly affect such plans or actions.

He is one who makes allowance for it as a real factor in life, whether to endeavour to neutralize its effects or to take advantage of its assistance as circumstances may permit and the case may demand.

Belief is not the mere mental or expressed assent to the truth of a statement, or the profession of acquiescence in the correctness of a definition, or approbation of the accuracy of a description, but the practical effect produced on the behaviour resultant from and consistent with the giving of such assent or acquiescence or approbation.

Belief is not the acknowledgment of the worthiness of any principle of action to be accepted as true, and adopted as a rule of life, but the line of conduct and action subsequent to, based on, and consistent with such an acceptance, and evidencing such an adoption.

It is, in short, not the mental or oral avowal of acceptance of a rule, but the conformity in action to its requirements.

To say this, is not to attach any fanciful or strained import to, much less to suggest or manufacture a forced or false signification for, a common word, but simply to call attention to its original and true meaning. The words *to believe*, really mean neither more or less than just to live as making allowance for.

However much in the course of successive generations, and in consequence of perhaps many and varied influences, the original and absolutely correct force of the nowadays seemingly so generally misunderstood, at all events so frequently apparently misapplied, expression *to believe* has been lost sight of, wrested, or perverted, it is still as clearly as ever manifest to any who will seek its meaning in its curt and simple derivation and composition.

The prefix 'be,' and the old Saxon verb *lifan*, to make allowance for, combine to form our well-known word 'belief.'

To how many minds the use of the word, even on some stray occasion, much less habitually, suggests any such meaning, is a question which may safely be left to the reader.

It is not taking up a false or perilous, though to many perchance it may appear a somewhat bold, not to say untenable position, to assert and boldly maintain that to the majority of minds the expression serves but to suggest or describe that mental action which recognizes any statement or description as true.

Upon the causes which may have led, or contributed, from time to time to the maintenance, adoption, and propagation of this error, it is not intended here at least to dilate.

It may be that one, if not the chief, reason is to be found in that tribute of common sense to the utility of truth, which would wish, for the credit of the human judgment, so indissolubly to associate the possession of knowledge with its beneficial employment as to willingly accept the admission, or profession, of having it as synonymous with a guarantee for its exercise.

It may also be that the displacing, for the purposes of religious worship, of the Saxon by the Roman tongue may have contributed in some degree to the subsequent misapplication of the term belief, as tending to associate it in the popular mind rather with a public declaration of opinion than a course and habit of life.

But whatever the causes, the result is patent enough. It is a sufficiently obvious truth that, to the generality of minds, the employment of the word belief is not suggestive of that life of action to which it pointed in the minds of those who called it into existence.

Still the force that is latent has not departed. It is still there, and may be employed as of yore and as a word capable, in the strength of this its original and true meaning, of expressing, as no other word in the language does or can equally well, the reception of doctrine combined with its appropriation for the purposes of guidance, and its exhibition, and it may be development, in practice, we would employ it in its native fulness and strength as the grand classifying characteristic of mankind.

Each individual member of the human race is, with regard to every subject within the ken of his knowledge, a believer or an unbeliever.

The fact of knowledge involves either belief or unbelief, wherever and whenever such knowledge is at all applicable to the requirements or circumstances of the use of life.

With regard to every subject within the ken of his knowledge, he either accepts it as an existence, with all its to him known properties, and frames his actions over which it can, in his judgment, possibly exert any influence, direct or indirect, accordingly, and so is a believer; or he does not so accept it or take account of its power, and is an unbeliever.

It is true he may be but a dubious and hesitating, it may even be a sceptical recipient of knowledge, and but a timid and halting follower of its precepts; still, if he be but a follower of its precepts in the actions of life, he is as truly a believer as his more robust comrade who, a ready and undoubting disciple in the school of wisdom, goes forth a steady, manly, even it may be, if need demand, an heroic exemplifier in practice of what he has there heard inculcated. Such is a believer.

On the other hand, the man who, whilst admitting, perhaps even professing, the truth of principles, by his neglect of their guidance slights the advantage to be derived from putting them in practice, or defies the danger consequent on their disregard, is, on every occasion on which he so acts, just as truly an unbeliever as he who openly and avowedly demurs to the truth, or admitting the truth doubts the efficacy, or granting both the truth and efficacy, despises and rejects the aid of some proffered enlightenment.

In either case the man is an unbeliever.

There is of course a difference betwixt these classes of unbelief, but it is one rather of character than of degree. The one may be characterized as an *illogical*, the other as a *logical* unbelief.

The man who professes to accept knowledge as true, is manifestly illogical in his unbelief. He who refuses to accept it as true is at least logical in refusing to act upon it.

But if the former is the illogical, it is at the same time, in some sense at least, the more hopeful of the two classes, as it is undoubtedly by far the more numerous. It may well be said that there is more hope of the illogical unbeliever abjuring his unbelief, from the mere fact of his being already in the position of admitted, perhaps even of boasted, possession of that groundwork upon which all belief, no matter what its subject, must of necessity be built, namely knowledge.

He has a vantage ground upon which to erect the temple of consistency, and so far at least may be said to be nearer the possession of belief.

But he who denies absolutely, from whatever cause, or on whatever ground, the truth, or even theoretical value, of that information whencesoever it may be derived which must precede action, and which must afford the basis for belief, is manifestly not even as yet capable if he could be supposed willing to believe.

He must accept and admit principles in order to be in a position to produce practice. Until he accepts and admits, he has nothing to put in practice, and it is an absolute impossibility for him to believe, which is simply a putting in practice of certain knowledge.

It may perhaps not be altogether out of place, or perhaps unnecessary, to recall to mind that belief may at times, from the very nature of its functions, appear on the surface, hardly at all an active operation.

Believing in its full and absolutely perfect action must of necessity and in reality consist in the maintenance of trustful quiet, the absence of personal exertion, the passive, so to speak, but perfectly satisfied and calculating dependence on work having been, or being at the time, accomplished by another, when the acceptance of facts and the consistent allowance for their existence and influence involve or require the absence of personal interference or demand the repose of such confidence.

Belief in full swing is often of necessity trust in representation.

It may often perforce consist in the quiet confidence of implicit dependence on work being accomplished by another.

Many are the instances of this which might be cited from everyday life occurrences. Life is full of them.

The shipmaster in the dark and troubled night, whilst, by the dim light of the uneasy lamp, he pores with anxious eye over the outspread chart, must all the while, in his calculations for safety, reckon upon the helmsman whom he has left at his post.

The assumption that he is then steering as directed, is as important a factor in the planned escape from reefs and breakers as the pilot's knowledge or the captain's skill.

Belief may often be but a course of quiet waiting. It must needs be whenever quiet waiting is the line of conduct demanded by due and consistent allowance for the power and influence of facts.

Nowhere is this species of belief more clearly exemplified than in the commencement of a Christian career.

There the beginning is found in the resting in the acceptance of a pardon and peace to be enjoyed only for the sake of the already long-since accomplished and once for ever finished all-sufficient sacrifice and labours of another.

Then the doing anything but accepting of that finished and perfect atoning sacrifice, as made for *oneself*, is sheer and absolute unbelief, because not acting in accordance with God's announcement of what is a matter of historical fact.

In that case the work of belief is to accept

that work as what it purports to be, complete in itself, and it is as much an act of belief to accept it as such and rest upon it for pardon, acceptance, and peace, as it is to perform any of those works of Christian love and charity which are at once its fruits, and the duties, as well as ornaments, of the subsequent life of faith.

And here it may be remarked, that as there is no field where the effects of error are of necessity more disastrous and appalling than in that of religion, so is there apparently no sphere of action where the misappreciation of the true force of the term, and misuse of the word belief has been more productive of disadvantage and injustice to the cause which above all others it ought to serve.

It may well be that much if not all of the acrimony of dispute which has from time to time arisen as to the true relative position of faith and works, might, at least in modern times, to a very large extent have been avoided, if not rendered impossible, because manifestly unnecessary, by a due attention and regard to the actual import of the word belief.

Many centuries ago the name Christian was given to those who not only accepted but believed the doctrines of apostolic teaching.

Those who then bore it were but few in number, now they are many, but it could hardly be said that at the present day all who boast the designation are, so far at least as apparent consistency of life is concerned, entitled to its possession equally with those to whom it was first appropriated.

Still, good, bad, or indifferent soldier of the cross, as each modern professor of Christianity may be, and separated by so many centuries from the veterans in the fight, the rules of warfare are identically the same for the modern Christian as for the primitive convert.

These rules are either stated absolutely and embodied in precise terms in the pages of Holy Writ, or if transmitted through any other medium, as derived from the same divine source, must be clearly logically reconcilable with the doctrines and teachings of the inspired page.

One of those, foremost, clear, and indispensable, is implicit reliance on the absolute infallibility of God's Word.

Now by the possession of absolute knowledge of the true and correct on any subject, we are in a position justly to detect as false, and stigmatize as erroneous, that which is clearly and diametrically opposed thereto.

In other words, if it is impossible to reconcile two principles or courses of action, and the one is known on indisputable authority to be undoubtedly and absolutely true, the other may safely be assumed to be as certainly false.

Now if it be found that there are certain principles with regard to the science and art of the upbringing of the young, either explicitly laid down or by fair and honest deduction clearly derivable from the sacred volume, it must follow that any pursuance of that science and art, in vogue in every-day practice, so far as repugnant to or irreconcilable with such principles, must be, no matter by whom followed, or by what specious pretensions of expediency, utility, or even apparent necessity it may be supported or defended, defective, unsound, false, and mischievous.

It need hardly be added that it must of necessity be the duty of every professing philanthropist, but above all of the Christian, the best because the only real and true, to express his dissent from any such, to oppose and hinder its carrying out, to reject its guidance for himself, and to prevent its acceptance, maintenance, and employment on the part of others to the utmost of his power.

CHAPTER II.

UPBRINGING.

IN every investigation which is to be conducted through the medium of language it is manifestly highly desirable, if not absolutely imperative, that strict attention should be paid to the accuracy of the language employed, and that, even when views are sought to be presented in what is known as a popular form, no affectation of simplicity of style should be allowed to operate, or be brought forward, as a pretext or excuse for inaccuracy of diction.

It seems therefore advisable, though even at perhaps very imminent risk of incurring the charge of pedantry, to adopt a perhaps rather unfrequently employed term as representative of the combined science and art to which our attention is to be directed. Whilst doing so, too, it may not perhaps be altogether out of place to state the reasons which have led to its adoption in preference to others more generally employed to designate the subject of our consideration.

The two words Instruction and Education, are very commonly employed as if they were synonymous.

They are used indifferently, to all appearance, to express that combined employment of the impartation of knowledge, of systematized direction and superintended exercise of the natural gifts and powers, and of that discipline of the moral faculties which all together are directed, as they are considered requisite, to the befitment and preparation of the young for their share in the business of life.

They would seem from their accepted promiscuous employment to convey to the minds of very many, if not of the majority, of those who so use them the same meaning. Whether this is so, and if it is so whether it arises from want of due consideration or from ignorance of their true respective significations, is of comparatively little moment. Their apparently indiscriminate use is an incontrovertible fact.

Now that their adoption as equivalent terms is

not strictly speaking justifiable, will readily appear on a reference to their respective derivations and true meanings. It must then appear manifest to the unbiassed mind that whatever use or misuse may be made of them, in popular converse, they actually point to, and ought to be employed to designate totally distinct, though at the same time most intimately connected, in fact it might truly be said in the ordinary run of cases inseparable, operations in one and the same great work.

They are, and must undoubtedly always be, joint factors in the training of mankind. But still they are not, correctly speaking, designative of the same thing, and ought not to be employed as if they were. The operations which they each denote are in their respective natures and immediate objects totally distinct, and ought not to be confounded.

Instruction, whatever its source, whether divine revelation, personal observation, inclusive of course of the fruits of experience, or that store of knowledge, whencesoever derived, already in the possession of others is an imparting of information.

Education is the development of power. The drawing out of that latent force which without the possession of knowledge would be unavailable.

That there should have arisen a laxity or confusion in their use is perhaps no very great wonder, when regard is had to the fact of their almost universal apparent inseparability.

Education is in fact almost an impossibility except as a result of the intervention of instruction. Of course it need hardly be added that it is scarcely possible to impart instruction without some amount of education being the result, unless in cases where the condition of the recipient is utterly and irretrievably abnormal.

This being so, it is easy to understand how education has come to be suggestive of precedent instruction, and instruction to seemingly involve as a matter of course, and necessary result, education.

The truth most probably is that when in the course of ordinary conversation either term is used, it actually calls up to the mind of the speaker, and is intended to convey to that of the hearer, a something combining both.

At all events, if such is not the intended effect of its employment, it is very frequently, perhaps almost invariably, the actual result of its use.

Whichever of the two words is employed, it serves to suggest the whole process of school training inclusive as well of that imparting of knowledge, necessary to render available the natural powers and capabilities of the individual, which is instruction proper, as that supplying, so far as may be, of those external circumstances of habit, direction, and discipline, most favourable to the successful development, fostered growth, and beneficial employment of the powers and capacities thus fitted for action and called into play.

Cultivation is a word which would seem under its figurative guise well and beautifully to represent the combined operation of instruction with education, which is so inadequately and improperly attempted by the use of either term alone.

By it we have truly and well depicted before the mind's eye the human soul, with all its latent powers and capacities, as a fair domain of virgin soil rich but as yet unproductive. By it we behold the utilizing seeds of knowledge buried beneath its surface. By it is suggested the nurturing care which watches over and tends the growing produce from the delicate green of the bursting germ till the full rich golden ear of harvest crowns and rewards the skill and industry and assiduous care of the satisfied and delighted husbandman.

And as the skill which wins its reward from the nurture of nature need not be confined in its exercise to the care of the bread-yielding harvest, but may find opportunity for its fostering solicitude, in the beauteous flowers or the luscious fruit, or may tend the handsome shrub, or rear the stately monarch of the dale, so this image of husbandry may be extended to represent the culture not only of the necessary and useful but of the superfluous and ornamental, and may with equal propriety be taken to depict the training which fits for the laborious handicraft as that which prepares for the senate or the field.

Yet it might be that its very comprehensiveness as a symbolic word should, in certain instances, operate as an objection to its employment; for as the tree, long after it has attained the age of fruitfulness and has contributed to the enrichment and gratification of man must still, in order to prolonged productiveness, remain the object of the husbandman's care, it must, in that instance at least, be regarded as hardly a faultless symbol of the care which is, strictly speaking, directly and purely preparative for life, and which has discharged its proper functions and yields its charge as the object of its solicitude steps down, all begirt for independent action, into the sounding arena of active life.

But if this consideration, of the comparatively brief period to which the task of preparing the young for entering upon the struggle of life must be confined, detracts from the absolute suitability of the figure of cultivation, as exactly suggestive of such work, it may also very well serve to point to the incorrectness of employing either of the terms instruction or education.

Although the preparation of youth must be sought as the result of a combination of what is strictly expressed by each of those terms, yet the time for their continued employment is limited to a certain number of years at a certain period of life, whilst the operation represented by either of these terms may be, in fact is, lifelong.

The whole earthly career of man, from the first dawn of infant intelligence to the eclipsing hour of death, is one prolonged course of instruction and education. To describe lifetime as one long term of schooling, were but to repeat a trite but commonplace aphorism.

It is indeed true that life is a school and lifetime a prolonged course of training, but as, in the juvenile growth of the individual, the simple teaching of the infant school is the manifestly natural prelude to the higher erudition of the academy, and as without the elementary preparation of the former the elaborate culture and finish of the latter were, if not absolutely unattainable, at least not to be very reasonably expected, so is it with regard to the training of the youthful in relation to the experimental acquisition of wisdom in riper years. It is not, however, with the lessons of mature manhood or ripe old age that we have to do, directly at least, in the course of the present considerations, but with that training of the youthful mind which is to prepare for the advantageous self-appropriation of such lessons.

To well describe such an undertaking, the simple word Teaching is certainly better adapted than instruction or education, employed separately, as serving to embrace both.

It is superior to the figurative expression cultivation as presenting in reality much of which the other is after all but a symbol.

But to best and most comprehensively, with at the same time a due regard to the efficacy and aid of the figurative, describe that process, in every particular adapted to its end, another term suggests itself.

The instruction which is indispensable, the education which is requisite, the love that nurtures, the discipline that curbs, the sympathy which encourages and cheers, and all else that may be supposed capable of contributing to befit the human unit for its place in the true and active economy of human life, appear most admirably comprehended and most amply expressed in the term Upbringing.

CHAPTER III.

THE BIBLE.

EVERY believer in Christ must of course accept the Bible as the enunciation of absolute truth.

The fact that it has directly, or by implication, the pledge of His veracity as a guarantee for its trustworthiness, is sufficient ground for such an one to regard its teachings as infallible.

To do otherwise seems so manifestly irreconcilable with a trust in His truthfulness as to lay any one, who so acts, open to a charge of want of confidence in his Master, which would be glaringly inconsistent enough in the case of the disciple of any teacher.

What Christ Himself accepted and referred to as true, and what His duly commissioned and inspired apostles taught or acknowledged as such, must surely be entitled to acceptance by every one who professes Him for Saviour and Lord.

The only question which could possibly arise to disturb the mind of such an one would be regarding the right of what passed current as the record or transcription of such truth to a place within the sacred volume.

Of course what might have unworthily found place amongst the writings of the inspired volume could not demand implicit obedience, though it might be entitled to a large amount of reverence and respect.

Once however fairly determined, through the medium of able and just criticism, as being, as it purported to be, duly entitled to a place amidst writings furnishing beyond a doubt the correct expression of the truth, it only remains to accept, acknowledge, and believe.

It could scarcely be unprofitable, and would perhaps be interesting, to review some of the reasons for the determination and acceptance of our popularly received canon of Scripture; but upon the historical or critical grounds for the absolute and unhesitating recognition of the claims to validity of that authority, to the judgment of which it is intended to submit the system in practice in too many cases of upbringing, it is not proposed to dilate.

To do so, although not inconsistent with, would certainly be unnecessary for our purpose. Composed as it is in part of those ancient scriptures which, handed down through successive generations, with reverential and devoted care, were in the course of time ratified by the personal authority, and sanctioned by the public use of Him to whom they bore witness; and in part of that collection of biography, history, doctrine, injunction, and prophecy which the almost unanimous decision of the Christian Church has from earliest centuries acknowledged and professed to accept as inspired, the canon of Holy Writ as adopted by the Reformed Protestant Churches of this country is that authority in faith, and instructor in morals, to the arbitrament of which we would appeal.

Assuming that the Bible must, as it does, furnish, either directly or indirectly, all instruction necessary for the government and direction of mankind in the discharge of every duty which can under any possible set of circumstances become incumbent, as it will in the fulfilment of even the most minute and varied relations arising in the most delicate and complex exigencies of the most refined civilization, it may of course be expected to provide ample guidance in the carrying out of that most momentous of undertakings, the upbringing of the young, that course of instruction and education and loving discipline whereby the body, soul, and spirit of the young human being is to be gradually fitted and prepared to take part in the conduct and business of life.

That it does so is as a matter of fact well enough known.

Many passages refer explicitly and directly to the training of youth. Many other incidentally afford insight with regard to, or indirectly proffer guidance on the subject.

Nor is there wanting abundance of that teaching by example of effects which is, in a sense, with some perhaps even more suggestive and efficacious than the instruction of precept. The historical and biographical portions of Holy Writ furnish this most plentifully.

The personal histories of the leading actors in successive generations, whether prominent for good or evil, depict in the beatific sheen of heaven's own approval, or display, illumined by the awful gleams of righteous judgment, or in the lurid dimness of despair, the good or ill effects which have followed the adoption of the true or the false in the ethics of early nurture.

More potent and momentous still, though only on account of their magnitude, the destinies of races and the fates of nations attest no less loudly, though to some perchance it may appear less manifestly, the dire effects of erroneous upbringing.

The weary servitude of Jacob, the tears of the poet king over a lost Absalom, the wail of breaking hearts from 'neath the willows by the far-off streams of Babylon, each tells a like tale.

But it is not with the examples, whether of success or failure, that we would have to do. It is, alas! indeed not necessary to turn to the pages of Holy Writ for testimony to the prolific qualities in sorrow and suffering of bad or even indiscreet upbringing. We have but to look around, thrice happy those who cannot find in their own circle; we have but to recall to mind instances which have from time to time come within our own observation, or been furnished by the annals of misery and crime to supply ourselves with saddest, and at the same time most palpable, evidence to a like effect, evidence of the appalling evils which may result from even incorrect, or injudicious, early training. But we must not digress. Upon the regions of the historical and biographical we would not enter, save it may be from time to time to cull an illustration.

It is with the doctrinal, the dogmatic, and the preceptive portions of Scripture that we must mainly have to do.

And yet, in the elimination from the pages of Holy Writ of a truly Christian scheme, theoretical and practical, of juvenile culture, attention is not of necessity, in truth cannot be, confined to the consideration of such passages as ostensibly point directly and specifically to the subject of our thoughts.

The Bible to be accepted as an authority and employed for the purposes of this investigation must be taken as a homogeneous, perfectly self-consistent, inter-dependent, and inter-elucidating declaration of what God would have mankind accept as the truth with regard to Himself, man, and existence.

It informs us of the attributes of God, of the origin, nature, characteristics, capacities, and destiny, actual or potential, so far as we are concerned to know, of man, of the end or purpose of the creation, not only of our world and race but of the universe, and how alone we can fulfil our part of contributing towards such end consistently with the enjoyment of absolute safety and true happiness, and it tells of the character, natural tendencies, influences, and powers at work in the world of morals, the real scene of our actions and the true field of our labours.

The Bible is the revelation of the salvation of our race.

It is the exponent of the story of the Cross.

The one great Sacrifice, its cause, its completion, its consequences, and its effects are its theme.

The Bible is too apt to be treated as a mere code of morality, open, so to speak, to the appropriation and obedience of all-comers.

It is not to be taken as such if morality is to be employed in the restricted sense in which it is commonly used.

That the Bible does furnish us with a system of morality, even in that narrow application of the word which is employed to signify conformity to those rules of, so to speak, moral police, the observance of which to some extent at least is absolutely necessary to render life comfortable, or even endurable, in the relations of man to man, and obedience to which is as necessary to personal comfort and temporal advantage as regard to the requirements of those physical laws which affect our corporeal wellbeing, is of course undeniable.

The Bible does indeed provide man with a code of rules for the government of his daily life in his transactions with his fellows, but not that it should be sought, as is too often the case, to extract such portions as bear upon the discharge of the relations of domestic and public life, and with them to endeavour to create a system, which is, as seems not unfrequently the case, to serve for the entire religion of life.

The morality of the Bible, using the word in its ordinary acceptation, was given to those in covenant with God.

We must not attempt to separate biblical morality from the cross of Christ.

The Cross is to be the *influencing cause* of our morality, just as without it we cannot attain to the highest morality, or rather it should be said to true, or absolutely perfect, morality.

The morality of the Bible is for us the morality of the Christian, and its acceptance the outcome and the fruit, or rather it should be said a portion, of our belief of the gospel, that is, in other words, of our framing our life in accordance with its tenets and requirements.

It cannot be too much borne in mind that the morality of the Bible, whether as regards the enactments of the Mosaic law or the injunctions of the gospel dispensation, were addressed to those already in covenant with God.

Nor ought it, as a consequence, to be forgotten that its requirements are to be viewed as directed to sanctification and not to justification, to the purifying and keeping pure, so far as the use of means is concerned in this world of sin and temptation, of the living temple of the consecrated being, or it may be further for its embellishment with such charms of grace, and truth, and purity, and loveliness, that those around may recognize, and acknowledge, and glorify the work of God.

It might be highly advantageous were the term morality generally employed in a far broader and more comprehensive sense, than as bearing merely upon an upright behaviour in the relations of this life. As under the moral law as applied to the tables of the Decalogue are comprehended all the duties of man to his Creator as well as to his fellow-creatures, it might well be employed as embracing reference to every duty consequent upon our position, not only in this world but the universe. With beautiful and perfect consistency the term might then be employed to stand for all the varied operations of the life of faith, and serve to depict not only the penitent and gladsome acceptance of the sole way of reconciliation with our God and Father, but all that subsequent life of Christian charity, the natural and ever, in some degree, inseparable resultant therefrom, which feeble and imperfect as it must needs often be, even in the case of the most gifted and favoured of believers, is yet for Christ's sake pleasing to heaven and beneficial to earth.

But even in adopting the usual and more restricted signification of the word which confines its application to the discharge of the varied duties and obligations of our race in the relationships of man to his fellows, we must ever guard against the fatal error of making, or even seeming to make, common cause with those who would attempt to separate the morality of the Bible from its connection with the cross of Christ.

We must ever avoid even the appearance of participating in that so fashionable, though not on that account needs it be said less flagrant, dishonesty which would strive to filch, to use no stronger expression, from the gospel the just and sole credit of those dogmas of purest and highest philanthropy, the origin of which, if not manifestly apparent in its direct teachings, is at least, on fair and candid consideration, easily traceable to them as its celestial source.

And in the use of Scripture for the purposes of our present investigation it is moreover never to be forgotten, as in fact it ought not to be overlooked in any reference to it for any purpose whatsoever, that those portions of the New Testament, the Apostolic Epistles directed to instruct the reader and student in the conformation of his life to the divine model and standard, were originally and primarily addressed to Christians.

They were not addressed to the world at large, but to communities or to individuals who had already, ostensibly at least, accepted and appropriated the message of pardon and peace.

The Epistles were letters of counsel and comfort to those who had already professedly fled for refuge to 'the hope set before them in the gospel.'

'All scripture is,' we full well know, 'given by inspiration of God, and is profitable for reproof and for instruction in righteousness,' and the believer is entitled so to use it; but still it is true that this very declaration of the all-pervading efficacy of the scriptures of the Old Testament is to be found set forth in an epistle to an early convert to Christianity.

It may doubtless appear to some that it is a work of supererogation to call attention to such matters as these, and that all the more especially considering the class of readers for whom these remarks are avowedly intended.

Yet, after all, placed as professing believers are in the midst of a country in the hands of an enemy, in a climate the very purest natural exhilarations of which are fraught with danger to the most careful of sojourners, surrounded by an atmosphere in which the pestilential miasmas of liberalism of indifference are too apt to be mistaken for the gentle zephyrs of heaven-born charity, and ever exposed to the insidious attacks of an infidelity no less decided, and no less dangerous, because it conceals its leprosy beneath the cloak of a considerate philanthropy, and professes acceptance of all that is kindly and benevolent in Holy Writ, though scornfully renouncing all allegiance to Him who gave it, there need after all be no great wonder if a few sentences should be devoted, even in a treatise addressed to *them* on a consideration of how the Bible ought to be viewed and employed.

It is truly neither sought nor wished by any of these remarks to even seem to arrogate the presumptuous or blasphemous position of attempting to define the possible extent of influence, or to ascribe any limit to the power, of a single word of Holy Writ. For one the touching pathos and heart-felt appropriateness of the Psalms, for another some rousing and soul-stirring denunciation of a Prophet, for another the graphic narrative of a Gospel, perchance the very words of our Blessed Lord and Saviour, for another the strong overwhelming logic of a Pauline Epistle, or for another the affectionate admonitions and encouragements of the loving Apostle may be the, humanly speaking, casual and fortuitous means employed by the Holy Spirit to awaken, or to strengthen, the spiritual life.

All that is sought is merely that a like due

attention to the circumstances and objects of its composition which ought, in the employment of all lawful means for its right and just comprehension, to be applied to any merely human composition, should be paid in the consideration of the Book of books. It can never be that the obedience of a believer to the injunction to be 'diligent in business' should be wrong, and to no employment could it by any possibility be more appropriately, or needfully, applied than in the perusal for instruction and guidance of the Word of God.

Such a diligent use of means is all that is herein besought.

CHAPTER IV.

MEANS.

HOWEVER unsatisfactory and unprofitable, though interesting and curious, as may always be any attempts to explain the phenomena of those conjunctions of successive events known in popular language under the denominations of causes and effects, the almost constant, if not perpetual, recurrence of their apparent connection affords sufficient justification for their anticipated relationship being treated as one of the grand agencies whereby the government of the world is carried on.

And just as the realized connection between cause and effect is indelibly impressed upon the human mind, so also is the conviction that in order to the attainment of any end it is necessary to employ means.

The employment of means to ends may be truly described as the most generally acknowledged principle for the government in their actions known to our race. And if the necessity for the employment of means be universally accepted and believed, so does there, also, exist the kindred impression, a knowledge strong and ready as instinct itself, that the means, in order to be of use, must be appropriate, and that in proportion to their adequacy will be the degrees of success to be anticipated as the result of their employment.

Whether the means are in the nature of language or of mechanism, whether the end in view be to rouse the enthusiasm of assembled thousands, or to pierce a pathway through the adamantine rock, it matters not, the mean must be suitable to the end.

The instrument must be adapted to do the work. Nay, further, it must not only be suitable for such work in general, but, in each individual instance, regard must be had to that species of such work which has to be undertaken, to the peculiar exigencies and special difficulties of the position. The skiff which would be perfectly well enough adapted for the placid waters of the lake would be but ill suited for the open sea, and utterly unfit for ocean, when the tempest burst upon its breast.

The principles upon which the suitability of an instrument is ever to be calculated must include considerations of its appropriateness for the work, together with due regard to any special difficulties which may be entailed, through the peculiar circumstances, if any, under which the labour has to be carried on.

Appropriateness for the work, together with a due regard to any special difficulties which may have to be encountered in its execution, whether they arise from the nature of the material to be operated upon, or from the peculiar circumstances under which the labour has to be carried on, must always be the test of the fitness of any instrument.

So any system of upbringing, to be truly efficacious in any degree, must be proportionately adapted to the situation, capacity, and requirements of the subject of its care *as they really are*.

That method which is intended to be truly efficacious to the utmost possible extent, must be fully adapted to the nature and requirements of man as they really are. Any plan by which it should be proposed to treat man as different to

D

what he is, or as existing under circumstances other than those amidst which he is in reality placed, must needs be erroneous; and its inadequacy will of necessity just be proportioned to the extent to which it ignores his true nature and capacities, or disregards the real facts of his position.

If, for instance, it openly and utterly denied the existence of the unseen world, or avowedly repudiated man's relations therewith, so as to ignore the possibility, not to say certainty, of his future existence being affected by his actions in the present life, no matter how advantageous, if such a thing were possible, such a system of upbringing might prove with regard to the affairs of time it would be inefficient, because inadequate, as not providing for more than the mere outset of a never-ending career.

Such a system, of course, would bear upon its face so manifestly the stigma of error that for those who were, in any sense, believers in the Christianity of the Bible it could be suggested but to be rejected.

For those to whom these remarks are avowedly addressed the witting adoption of such a system of upbringing would seem almost impossible.

Yet although ready enough to repudiate, and that too with generous warmth, the possibility of looking favourably upon, much less of adopting, any school which ignored a due regard to the endless future, it is possible from the force of surrounding circumstances, of political association, of that influence ofttimes most insidious when least suspected, the consequence of evil example, or of unhallowed alliance, and last not least of the plausible pleadings of self-satisfying expediency, to seem, at least, not altogether unaffected by the varied sophistries with which it is sought to support a purely secular system of public instruction.

Moreover, whilst manifestly, not to say professedly, atheistical schemes are not to be supposed capable of consideration, much less of approval or adoption, there is still after all a possibility, through the *partial or improper* application of biblical principles and injunctions, of pursuing, it may be so to speak unconsciously, a course which, whilst not perhaps absolutely incompatible with true, at the same time falls far short of full and consistent, belief of the gospel teaching.

To truly and correctly gauge the fitness of any instrument, it is necessary to be in the possession of accurate and sufficient knowledge of the nature and properties of the matter to be operated upon, of the character and object of the work to be performed, of any circumstances calculated to affect favourably or detrimentally the progress of the undertaking, and also of the capabilities of the instrument itself to operate upon such material, in such a case, for such an end, to a successful issue.

Now, applying this principle to the subject of upbringing, it follows, in order to our being able to form a right judgment as to the true possible efficacy of any proposed system, that we must be in possession of accurate knowledge as to the nature, properties, tendencies, and capabilities of young humanity, of the real, ultimate, and supreme object of the work to be performed upon it, of the nature of the surroundings amidst which such work is to be carried on, and of the ability of the proffered mode of procedure so to accomplish such an undertaking.

With regard to every one of these particulars it is of course to the Bible that we must turn for sufficient, and absolutely reliable information and judgment. We shall find all we seek in these respects, nor that alone.

Not only shall we be enabled to discern, and that beyond a doubt, if any on the subject could ever have existed in our minds, that the only scheme, by any possibility appropriate to our requirements, must be one which can justly come under the denomination of a religious course of upbringing, but, beyond that, we shall be furnished with the details of the *only* system which actually exists sufficient for all the exigencies of our position, and, furthermore, we shall find ample instructions for our guidance in its application and employment.

It might appear to many quite unnecessary to occupy time by more than a mere passing reference to the familiar Evangelical doctrines as to the nature of man, the end of his being, and the character of his moral surroundings; and so it would be were the credence of Divine Revelation which characterizes all who may peruse these pages in the case of each individual equally full and unqualified.

But belief where actually present, and that to such an extent as to avail its possessor for the purpose of accepting all that is necessary for the enjoyment of personal salvation, may be in further respects of such various degrees of fulness, and so affected by a variety of influences, internal and external, that there may be many true Christians, whose views, with regard to each of these very subjects of faith, may be erroneous to an unthought of and alarmingly dangerous extent.

Nor can such deficient or incorrect views with regard to such matters of doctrine be, in every case, truly described as either involuntary misapprehension, or error of judgment, though springing perhaps most frequently, if not always, from the same source as the latter, so called, class of mistakes generally does.

Errors of judgment, as they are popularly styled, are probably most frequently, if not almost invariably, the result of inadequate knowledge rather than of the mistaken, though honest, application of sufficient information.

A man, for instance, is said to have misjudged his distance from the target or the shore; he has, *in fact*, been too careless or too self-confident to use the recognized means at his disposal to measure it with certainty and accuracy, and the failure to win a prize, or the loss of a ship, is the consequence.

The true cause is ignorance, and that, moreover, culpable, because avoidable.

So is it probably in the majority of the cases above alluded to.

The knowledge of the spiritual is to be obtained through the teaching and under the guidance of revelation, and a failure to accept and follow those views which it affords of man, and his concernments in reference thereto, is probably in the majority of cases of error on the part of professing Christians really attributable to the neglect of the study of what Scripture says on the subject. That there may exist in the carrying out of the details of Christian life, room for great variety of opinion, and as it may appear quite fair occasion for much diversity in action, is of course undoubted, nor may such difference of opinion or in behaviour be after all of any very great practical moment or, on the whole, otherwise than beneficial.

But it is far different with regard to the acceptance and belief of matters of such fundamental importance as the right and just conception of man's natural sinfulness and inability for any good, the perpetual recognition of the true end of his, as of all, created existence, and of the necessarily hostile influences of the world and its belongings, no matter how apparently modified in the semi-consecration of a nominally Christian civilization.

Necessary to a just appreciation of the benefits of the gospel, and advantageously borne in mind in the practical application of its truths and principles of action to the upbringing of the young, as the full acceptance of the absolute and infallible utterances of the Word of God on these subjects must needs ever be, it is manifestly very advisable that for the purposes of these considerations our views with regard to such utterances should be brightened and our memories refreshed by some direct reference to the clear and explicit language of Scripture.

Such a course it is now intended presently to follow.

CHAPTER V.

HUMAN NATURE.

IN a reference to those words of Holy Writ which describe that nature, with all its inherent properties, tendencies, and capabilities, in the possession of which man is ushered upon his never-ending existence, and which, however subsequently affected by the miraculous operation of the second birth, still to the end of this present life never fails to exercise a more or less potent influence upon its possessor, it is very natural that our opening quest should lead us to those portions of Scripture which detail or elucidate the early history of our race.

Of the sad day whereon the leafy groves and pleasant glades of Eden beheld that act of disobedience, by which the parents of mankind involved their offspring in all the weary troubles, and direful consequences, of the fall, it is unnecessary to speak at length.

The warning disregarded, the commandment disobeyed, the covenant broken, simultaneously with the triumph of unbelief, commenced the reign of spiritual and corporeal death. Man's history was thenceforth to be one long testimony to the existence, presence, and power of evil.

If in those early antediluvian days, as in later centuries, there were those who, in the pride of their hearts, were prone to doubt the full weight and true force of the calamity which had befallen our race, and to question if man were altogether so fallen and so vile as the voice of faith declared, it was not very long ere the testimony of Heaven was supported by the evidence of manifested facts.

Not bereft, whatever else had been lost or impaired, of an ample measure of energy and power, these were thenceforth to be, alas! too frequently grievously misapplied, and as each succeeding generation advanced in experience and attainments, so also was there a growth in wickedness ever more and more regardless and atrocious.

Not many had come and gone, ere at the Divine command, the sole prophet of faith, the believing

Noah, prepared that ark which was to receive him and his charge amid the overwhelming devastation of the deluge, and we find recorded in the Mosaic narrative that:—

'God saw that the wickedness of man was great in the earth, and that every imagination of the thought of his heart was only evil continually' (Gen. vi. 5).

But God's promise must stand, and the gift of faith fitted the chosen instrument to preserve creation's being through the otherwise universal destruction. 'Mid tempest and desolation the ark rode in safety on the waters.

Forth from their long seclusion, those twelve months' discipline of hope and expectation, came the rejoicing patriarch and his household, and the altar had been reared, and the sweet savour of the sacrifice had ascended, and God's blessing once more came down upon the rejuvenescent earth when we read:

'The Lord said in His heart, I will not again curse the earth any more for man's sake; for the imagination of man's heart is evil from his youth' (Gen. viii. 21).

How soon was a sad evidence of the presence of

sin to be furnished in the domestic history of that very family which had been so lately and so wonderfully preserved! Years had elapsed since the bow of promise had girt the Eastern sky, and in distant Edom as the most patient of men bemoaned in theophilosophic plaint the infirmity and transiency of earthly life, there falls upon the ear his sad but true testimony to the secret of human woe :

'Who can bring a clean thing out of an unclean? Not one' (Job xiv. 4).

And kindred in nature was the response of his not too kind, or just, or sympathetic comforter, as the Temanite replied with the equally sad and true inquiry:

'What is man, that he should be clean? and he which is born of a woman, that he should be righteous?' (Job xv. 14).

Pass next to that home of bitter sorrow, the palace of David.

The inherent evil that had lain hid in germ in that very breast, which strong in faith had so dauntlessly and so oft defied the armies of the aliens, and which, so rich in piety and adoration, had hymned so many a song of loving praise and burning devotion, in an unguarded moment has asserted its power, and the hands of Judah's king have been imbrued in the blood of his faithful adherent.

And now, in the hallowed atmosphere of a soul-chastening penitence, as the forgiven but humbled spirit can look in sorrow, but in calmness, upon the awful and bitter past, what a testimony to our natural depravity are these familiar words in that Psalm, the comfort in successive centuries of so many a sin-weeping soul!

'Behold, I was shapen in iniquity; and in sin did my mother conceive me' (Ps. li. 5).

Shall we consult the inspired wisdom of the sagest of men? it is but to read:

'Who can say, I have made my heart clean, I am pure from my sin?' (Prov. xx. 9).

Passing on to the era of the greater prophets, in the days of Josiah, amidst the warnings of Jeremiah against the backslidings and idolatries of his erring countrymen, we find the declaration of the inborn evil of our nature in that all-comprehensive and universally-applicable passage:

'The heart is deceitful above all things, and desperately wicked: who can know it?' (Jer. xvii. 9).

Out of the days of types and shadows, of prophecies since more or less completely fulfilled, from chronicles of past history, and from soul experiences of departed saints, come we now to the declaration of Him ' who spake as never man spake.' Following hard upon denunciation of those vain traditions wherewith Pharisaic hypocrisy had overlaid, concealed, and nullified the spirit of the law, and affording explanation to the inquiring disciples of that warning parable that had just fallen upon the ears of the gathered throng, He, who knoweth all things, thus declared the heart of man the prolific source of every form of evil.

' From within, out of the heart of man, proceed evil thoughts, adulteries, fornications, murders, thefts, covetousness, wickedness, deceit, lasciviousness, an evil eye, blasphemy, pride, foolishness' (Mark vii. 21, 22).

The great sacrifice once for ever accomplished, and the atonement complete, what testimony to the natural vileness of humanity is supplied by those apostolic writings which demonstrate the necessity for, elucidate the systematic structure, and explain the operation of the gospel remedy? Let us take the Epistle to the Romans, where with all the overwhelming force of an irrefutable logic the necessity for, as well as the manner of the operation of our salvation, together with the method of its appropriation by the individual is set forth.

In the list of transgressions into the commission of which mankind are described as having fallen, consequently upon their having been given up to vile affections as a result of their unbelief in the Creator's eternal power and Godhead, may be found ample illustration of the corruption of our nature, with its inherent debasing tendencies and capabilities for evil.

Superadded to uncleanness and vile affections, we find the human soul described as under the guidance of a reprobate mind:

'Being filled with all unrighteousness, fornication, wickedness, covetousness, maliciousness; full of envy, murder, debate, deceit, malignity; whisperers, backbiters, haters of God, despiteful, proud, boasters, inventors of evil things, disobedient to parents, without understanding, covenant-breakers, without natural affection, implacable, unmerciful' (Rom. i. 29, 30, and 31).

Nor does the particularization of wickedness stop here, for a little further on, after the Jew despite the hereditary advantages, spiritual and moral, involved in or attached to his position as the chosen guardian of the oracles of God has been proved under sin together with the Gentile, as if the above referred to category of evil had not been sufficiently comprehensive, the denunciation of the sinfulness common to both goes on to declare:

'There is none righteous, no, not one: There is none that understandeth, there is none that seeketh after God. They are all gone out of the way, they are together become unprofitable; there is none that doeth good, no, not one. Their throat is an open sepulchre; with their tongues they have used deceit; the poison of asps is under their lips: Whose mouth is full of cursing and bitterness: Their feet are swift to shed blood: destruction and misery are in their ways: And the way of peace have they not known: There is no fear of God before their eyes' (Rom. iii. 10–18).

Then after the glorious announcement of that righteousness of God, which is freely given as the sole and sufficient ground of justification for those whose spiritual taint and impotency must for ever preclude any other mode of satisfaction, we find the sad and solemn truth as to the universal condition of man by nature, since the fall, thus all-comprehensively summed up:

'All have sinned' (Rom. iii. 23).

Passing on to that chapter of peace and hope and comfort, wherein, starting from the previously fully demonstrated conclusion that it is through justification by faith that we have peace with God, the Apostle goes on to show how if reconciled whilst enemies, much more being reconciled we shall be saved as friends, and so sheds the golden radiance of a heaven-given hope down into the dreary glooms and yawning chasms and appalling depths of the valley of tribulation, we find the whole doctrine of original sin explicitly laid down:

'As by one man sin entered into the world, and death by sin; and so death passed upon all men, for that all have sinned' (Rom. v. 12).

And, before we have thus far advanced in the chapter whence this last quotation is derived, we have passed the verse which tells it was:

'When we were yet without strength,' that, 'in due time Christ died for the ungodly' (Rom. v. 6).

See too, when describing the attitude of opposition on the part of the carnal mind, an opposition how utterly invincible by merely human strength it needs hardly be said, against the renewed will of the regenerated and struggling spiritual nature, with what evidence as to the utter helplessness for good of poor fallen humanity are we furnished in the declaration:

'For I know that in me (that is, in my flesh) dwelleth no good thing: for to will is present with me; but how to perform that which is good I find not' (Rom. vii. 18).

Nor is this opposition an occasional outbreak, or rarely occurring act of rebellion; it is a condition of hostility so uniform and abiding as to be denominated a law:

'I find then a law, that, when I would do good, evil is present with me' (Rom. vii. 21).

This the product of 'sin that dwelleth in me' (Rom. vii. 20).

Then again, as to the mind which some in all the arrogant presumption of a blinded and intoxicating intellectual pride would have mankind regard as supremely qualified to be the unerring judge of the very essentials and qualities of virtue itself; how very different the judgment of Divine truth when the attitude of this self-same mind is described in such words as these:

'The carnal mind is enmity against God: for it is not subject to the law of God, neither indeed can be' (Rom. viii. 7).

Such the evidence derivable from the Epistle to the Romans, and similar in tenour is that adducible from any other of the succeeding letters to the Church. Take for example the message to that church which the great Apostle of the Gentiles had founded in the luxurious capital of Achaia.

It is to those citizens of the busy Corinth that the declaration, so obnoxious, in the incomprehensibility of the truth which it contains, to the native pride of the human intellect, is addressed.

'The natural man receiveth not the things of the Spirit of God: for they are foolishness unto him: neither can he know them, because they are spiritually discerned' (1 Cor. ii. 14).

The Galatians are told that

'The Scripture hath concluded all under sin' (Gal. iii. 22).

They are moreover also reminded of that strong animosity and rebellious struggling of the flesh against the spirit, to which such clear and pointed reference has been already met with in the Epistle to the Romans:

'The flesh lusteth against the spirit' (Gal. v. 17).

And then when in subsequent verses the works of the flesh are particularized, is the enumeration less humbling in its broad-stretching comprehensiveness, than any that has been already elsewhere given ?

'Now the works of the flesh are manifest, which are these: adultery, fornication, uncleanness, lasciviousness, idolatry, witchcraft, hatred, variance, emulations, wrath, strife, seditions, heresies, envyings, murders, drunkenness, revellings, and such like' (Gal. v. 19, 20, and 21).

If testimony, peculiarly striking on account of the literal correspondence of the very language, wherein it delineates the state of the unconverted, with the absolute terms of the dire predicted consequences of the fall, is required, it may be found in that passage of the Epistle to the Ephesians wherein the quickened erst-time worshippers of the goddess Diana are addressed as those

'Who were dead in trespasses and sin' (Eph. ii. 1).

How, too, the sin-degraded understanding, and the innate spiritual ignorance of our race is pointed to in the subsequent passages where those same once votaries of idolatry, now enfranchised children of the light, are admonished that they

'Henceforth walk not as other Gentiles walk, in the vanity of their minds; having the understanding darkened, being alienated from the life of God through the ignorance that is in them, because of the blindness of their heart' (Eph. iv. 18).

'That ye put off concerning the former conversation the old man, which is corrupt according to the deceitful lusts; and be renewed in the spirit of your mind' (Eph. iv. 22 and 23).

'For ye were sometimes darkness' (Eph. v. 8).

In the fond and uncensuring Epistle of the imprisoned Apostle to his beloved Philippians, those first-fruits of his European labours, amidst all that is so commendatory of the steadfast zeal and overflowing love of those whom he addresses, even there we must needs find a reference to 'our vile body' (Phil. iii. 21).

In the Epistle to the church at Colosse we read:

'Giving thanks unto the Father . . . who hath delivered us from the power of darkness' (Col. i. 12 and 13).

'And you, that were sometime alienated and enemies in your mind by wicked works' (Col. i. 21).

'And you, being dead in your sins and the uncircumcision of your flesh' (Col. ii. 13).

'Mortify therefore your members which are upon the earth; fornication, uncleanness, inordinate affection, evil concupiscence, and covetousness, which is idolatry' (Col. iii. 5).

That passage in one of the Epistles to Timothy wherein his father in Christ foretells:

'That in the last days perilous times shall come. For men shall be lovers of their own selves, covetous, boasters, proud, blasphemers, disobedient to parents, unthankful, unholy, without natural affection, truce-breakers, false accusers, incontinent, fierce, despisers of those that are good, traitors, heady, high-minded, lovers of pleasures more than lovers of God; having a form of godliness, but denying the power thereof' (2 Tim. iii. 1 to 5), may at first sight appear somewhat inappropriate as a proof of the capacities and potentialities for evil of our fallen nature, as having been, when originally penned, prophetic of the future, not descriptive of the past.

But the inspiration which imparts to the revealed word of Him, who is 'the same yesterday, to-day, and for ever,' that intrinsic and essential quality of absolute truth, which the mere accident of time cannot affect, and which renders the visions of prophecy as reliable as the records of accomplished fact can amply justify its employment.

Nor, if it might be added in all lowliest reverence and sincerest charity, if such a reason were wanting, could the evidence of our own senses as to the already sufficiently marked realization of its alarming and saddening enough picture, in the public and private condition of these our own times, fail to afford sufficient grounds for its acceptance.

Amid the words of counsel addressed to Titus when entrusted with the rule of the Cretan Church, we read:

'Unto them that are defiled and unbelieving is nothing pure; but even their mind and conscience is defiled' (Tit. i. 15).

All that poor, fallen, weak, unheaven-taught human nature has as monitor of good and evil, as arbiter of right and wrong, as judge of virtue and vice, itself impure and defiled.

It is surely unnecessary to adduce any further testimony from Scripture upon these points. The above-cited passages may well suffice to show how absolutely the Word of God testifies to the fallen nature, sinful properties, corrupt tendencies, and perverted capacities of our race. There has been supplied, as it appears, ample evidence of the existence and influence of that natural depravity, and impotency for good, which, demanding as it does the superhuman and miraculous resources of the gospel remedy, can always point to the very absoluteness of the necessity for such a salvation, as the strongest and most conclusive testimony to the natural character and exigencies of poor, fallen, lost humanity.

CHAPTER VI.

THE END OF EXISTENCE.

HAVING obtained, from the unerring page of Scripture, knowledge so specific and absolute, and evidence so incontrovertible as to the nature, properties, tendencies, and capabilities of that spirit and soul, which though acting but indirectly in relation to the external world, through the medium of a material body, and at the same time affected and influenced in a way and to a degree which to our finite comprehensions, and limited knowledge, is simply absolutely incomprehensible, by their connection with this same in itself so wondrous organic structure, are themselves, after all, the real and actual human unit, the immortal being, for which even eternal perdition brings no cessation of existence, it next remains to consider the true, ultimate, and supreme object of all the work to be performed upon them in the carrying out of the undertaking of the upbringing of the young.

Manifestly the immediate object of spiritual and mental instruction, education, nurture, and discipline, together with all else that may be deemed necessary to the right and successful conduct of this undertaking, must be so far analogous with the direct ostensible purpose of a merely physical uprearing, that it must be directed to the utilization, perchance development, of ability and power.

Such utilization or development, as the case may be, must again, in turn, be intended to enable, fit, or better qualify for the fulfilment or discharge of some real or imaginary accepted and recognized purpose of existence. If then we can arrive with absolute certainty at the knowledge of the crowning purpose of man's creation, we shall have therein presented to us that supreme object towards the fulfilment of which all life's labour ought in reason to be directed, and towards which by necessary implication all measures necessary or calculated to qualify for, or facilitate in the prosecution of, such labours should be made not only subservient to, but, so far as may be, convergent.

Now we do know the purpose of man's creation.

The all-inclusive object for which he was called into being, and for which he is sustained in existence, is the glory of God.

He may labour in love, or he may toil in hate, but for this he exists.

He may be a devoted servant, or a proud and defiant rebel, but whether in grateful obedience or in despiteful contempt, by submission or in rebellion, he must glorify his Creator.

That prayer which from thousands of worshipping assemblies in cloistered minster, or grey old church, or floating temple on the heaving breast of ocean, rises in common supplication on the solemn stillness of each returning Christian Sabbath, and in which it is besought that the godly, righteous, and sober life may be to the glory of God's holy name, full well embodies in its language of suppliant reconsecration the true supreme and all-embracing object of human existence.

So too that most methodical compendium of doctrinal and practical Christianity, the clear strong teachings of which may well have trained full many a martyr for his lonely slumber by the dark tarn or on the silent moor, and which, though penned by English Puritans, has become indissolubly associated with the foster land of its adoption, and to the influence of which, direct and indirect, the sons of Scotland owe an untold debt, commences its pre-eminently well systematized course of instruction with the announcement of the chief end of man as the glorifying of God.

By such chief end must needs be understood what has been above described as the supreme, paramount, and all-embracing purpose of our being, for it may not be suggested that man could exist for other ends or objects independent of, or apart from, that of God's glory.

To that all the ends and aims incident to the necessities or conditions of his existence, all his labours, all his sorrows, all his joys, his little achievements of the passing hour, bringing it may be in their train comfort and satisfaction to him-self, and happiness to others, in short, all his intermeddlings with and share in the conduct of the affairs of time, must be subordinate and contributory.

And subordinate and contributory they are and shall ever be, irrespective of whether they are the outcomes and accompaniments of the life of willing service of the through grace devoted bondsmen of

Divine Love, or the enforced or unconscious or hateful tribute to overpowering necessity, of those whom no reconciliation by the blood of the cross has brought into that relationship to their Almighty Father, which must needs precede the production of the fruits of acceptable worship.

Yet for those to whom these remarks are especially addressed, it is neither necessary, or perhaps otherwise worth while, to dilate upon the position of the unbelieving world in these matters, or of the subordination of evil to the purposes of almighty power.

The service which is to be consistent with the profession of belief, must needs be the willing adoration, characteristic of a consecrated life.

If those who profess to be believers fail to at least strive, according to the grace given them, to fulfil to the utmost the true supreme end of their being, it must be the result of weakness, sloth, inadvertence, or ignorance.

For those professing to acknowledge in all things the authority of their Creator and Redeemer, the dicta of divine truth, the inspired expression of heavenly wisdom, is in itself sufficient, at least ought to be, without pausing to reason further of the incontestable right of the Deity and Creator to the perpetual and entire services of those whom He has called into being and maintains in existence, or turning aside to consider the manifestly necessary logical sequences, in such respects, of the acceptance of the comparatively vague and indistinct shadowings of even the most philosophical development of any so-called natural theology.

For the professing believer it should be sufficient to recall to mind that

'The Lord hath made all things for Himself, yea even the wicked for the day of evil.'

Accepting then God's glory as the end of man's existence, embracing everything therein involved, and acknowledging it as the absolutely certain and necessary result of the accomplishment of the earthly career of every descendant of Adam, whether it has been a life of faith or of unbelief, it follows that for the avowed believer in Christ it is not only an incumbent, because commanded, duty, but the natural outcome of the exercise of sanctified and enlightened common sense, that in the course of belief there should be employed every lawful means available for the most thorough attainable development of all the capabilities of life, as subordinate and directed to that end, in the acceptance of the gospel.

In other words, the process of upbringing of the young, being intended for their beneficial and most truly advantageous employment of the occasions and opportunities of life, should be directed to their utilization of such occasions and opportunities for the glory of God, and that in the character of willing instruments.

Accepting the apostolic injunction to the Corinthian Church as the correct epitome of aim for the Christian life, the true ethical ideal of the regenerated existence is briefly announced:

'Whether therefore ye eat or drink, or whatsoever ye do, do all to the glory of God.'

To get the child, a born enemy of and rebel against the God of his fathers, converted into a loving and obedient subject of his Saviour and King, and thereafter so to train his early years and guide his growing powers as to prepare for and aid in the gradually advancing development of a life of faithful service, is in short, whether so recognized or not, for the Christian parent the supreme, and ever to be steadily regarded object of all upbringing.

It is not of course for a moment hereby suggested

that any mere human agency, however earnest, well intentioned, or well directed may be its endeavours, can take the place of, or in any degree operate as a substitute for that direct and miracle-working operation of the Almighty Spirit, without whose quickening, regenerating, sustaining, and directing influence the most sincere, hearty, and zealous endeavours, and the most patient and assiduous toil may be lavishly expended with no apparent result, much less be rewarded with any meed of manifest success.

Attention is only hereby called to that line of action which the believing parent or guardian of youth, as the honoured worker together with God, is not only permitted but called upon to pursue.

It is for such an one to use the means, available for and proper to the work in hand, in prayerful and firm dependence on the Divine faithfulness and promised blessing.

Now all this merely goes to show that the exigencies of the case demand that the first subject of instruction for the young should be with regard to God and the things of the unseen world; in other words, that the imparting of religious knowledge should precede all secular instruction.

This may seem, taken in its absolute, and, intentionally so expressed, uncompromising entirety, a very strong, perhaps even impracticable position to take up.

Such it may at first sight appear, yet neither its untoward strength nor apparent impracticability can alter the truth which underlies, or diminish the absoluteness of the necessity which supports it.

Before human life can be made what it ought to be, in accordance with the requirements of Christianity, one prolonged course of acceptable service, the worshipper must be accepted and consecrated for the work.

Now the one cardinal doctrine of the cross which lies at, and is, in fact, the foundation of the gospel, and which is so to speak the very reason and necessity for its being, is that there is but one way of acceptance with our Creator and God, that namely, through the one finished sacrifice of our Blessed Lord and Saviour Jesus Christ on Calvary as our substitute. So that the knowledge of the gospel salvation must, in accordance with the reasonable exercise of enlightened common sense, be of absolute necessity the first knowledge proper to be imparted to the youthful mind, in the reasonable employment of the only means capable of fitting its possessor for even commencing the Christian career.

Now there are it is to be apprehended many, perhaps very many, amongst professing believers, who, whilst willing enough to agree with the absolute necessity of religious instruction being made the foundation for all other, would hardly go so far as to be ready to accede to the demand that such instruction should consist of neither more nor less than the opening up to the youthful mind of the gospel plan of salvation *by substitution*. Many would candidly enough doubt the feasibility of such a course. Many others would seriously and honestly call in question its propriety. The dubiousness of the former would seem to arise from insufficient appreciation of the simplicity of the gospel.

The hesitation of the latter from inadequate realization of the absolute necessity for its acceptance *in all its fulness* at first and at once.

The bare possibility of either attitude being maintained by any professing believer, whether attributable to unsound teaching or to deficiency in personal experience of the action of the knowledge of the truth as it is in Jesus, might well afford sufficient excuse for the otherwise seeming impertinence of presuming to call attention to a brief consideration of what the gospel remedy truly is in regard to some of its details.

But when to a sense of the undeniable possibility is superadded, as the result of observation and experience, the deeply rooted conviction of the widespread entertaining of such views, ample justification may be pleaded for the adoption of such a course.

CHAPTER VII.

THE GOSPEL.

WHEN in the darkness of the Philippian dungeon the terrified keeper, restrained from the suicide of despair by the reassuring voice of the imprisoned Apostle, came trembling and bewildered to seek on bended knees the knowledge of safety, he was told, 'Believe on the Lord Jesus Christ.'

The same remedy which was applicable then to the requirements of that jailer is still, and must ever remain till the end of time, the only specific for the spiritual necessities of our race.

Now, what is it to believe on the Lord Jesus Christ?

Bearing in mind the true force and signification of the word believe, it may be described as to accept of what is told us in Scripture of the Lord

Jesus Christ, and so to act as to make allowance for it as really true, in its relations to and bearings on the exigencies of one's own individual case.

Of all the passages of Scripture which might occur to the student of Holy Writ as aptly suggestive in few words of the ultimate object of that mission of love which brought down our blessed Lord and Saviour to toil, suffer, and die for the children of men, perhaps none could be selected as more succinctly setting forth and embodying it than that portion of the Epistle to the Romans, wherein attention is directed to the 'gift of God' as being 'eternal life through our Lord Jesus Christ.'

The knowledge that eternal life *is* the gift of God through our Lord Jesus Christ, is in truth the burden of the gospel message, just as the conferring it upon those who will accept it is the object of the gospel remedy in its application and operation.

It is in the acceptance as true and the appropriation to each individual case of the provisions of that remedy that we exercise and manifest our belief in the Lord Jesus Christ.

The history of the original promise of this gift, and the facts relative to the provisions of its manifestation, acceptance, and enjoyment may be briefly summed up and recounted as follows.

All mankind through the disobedience of their first parents Adam and Eve, have been, are, or will be born in a fallen, guilty, ruined, and so far as regards any innate capability or self-attainable power of extricating themselves utterly and irretrievably lost condition.

God their Heavenly Father, the Almighty Creator of all things, who 'delighteth in mercy,' but 'is of purer eyes than to behold iniquity,' and who 'cannot look upon sin but with abhorrence,' and who though 'the Father of mercies' can 'by no means clear the guilty,' of His amazing love promised a way of salvation, whereby whilst every demand of Divine justice could be fully and absolutely satisfied, pardon, and peace, and His Divine favour might be enjoyed by His poor fallen and helpless creatures 'without,' so far as they in their own persons should be concerned, 'money' or 'price,' through and solely on account of the labours and sufferings of an appointed and accepted Substitute.

The accomplishment of this wondrous plan of salvation has been brought about through the gift and agency of His only-begotten Son, the same by whom the world had been created.

He having stooped to assume, for the purpose of substitution, a perfect and real human nature of true, but sinless flesh and blood, wrought out through an earthly career of humility, toil, anguish, and suffering, a spotless, perfect, and meritorious righteousness for all who should be willing to accept it, a righteousness far more than ample in its Divine superabundancy to satisfy every exaction of the highest and most inexorable demands of the Divine justice.

He concluded this life of substitutionary suffering, service, and meritorious action by offering up of Himself a full and sufficient sacrifice for the sins of the whole world, and thus became the author of eternal salvation to all them that 'believe on Him.'

Consigned to an earthly tomb, in the fulfilment of the predictions of prophecy, He was raised again by the Almighty Father in token of the acceptance of His finished work of suffering representation.

The great propitiation completed and its acceptance manifested, He ascended to the skies, possessor of all power in heaven and on earth, and now reigns at the right hand of power, Protector, Mediator, Ruler, and Representative of all that come to God through Him, that put their trust in Him as their Saviour and their God.

Exalted on high, He now vouchsafes the wondrous gift of His Almighty Spirit to awaken, and draw to Himself and then, leading in the footsteps of His example, to fit the pardoned, and justified, and consecrated sinner for a service of love and devotion on earth, and an abode in the realms of eternal glory hereafter. Nor would any synopsis, however brief, of the glorious gospel of the grace of God be complete without directing the thoughts to that grand consummation, the triumphant reappearing of our Lord and Redeemer when, returning in the awful solemnity of the last great day, He shall come again in the clouds of heaven to judge the quick and the dead, to justify before men and angels those whom He long ago purchased with His most precious blood, and kept, led, and sanctified by His eternal Spirit.

Now in this mighty and most wondrous scheme the all-predominant characteristic is freeness, and the all-pervading principle is substitution.

All the benefits of the gospel are the results of substitution.

This is true no less of the indirect effects of its reception than of the direct.

It is the case with regard to the enjoyment of the covenant blessings, which are conferred upon the believer in the course of his life of imperfect but filial obedience and consecrated service, as much as with reference to those more striking benefits, which are the accompaniments, or rather simultaneous adjuncts of his first repentance, approach to, and reconciliation with his Heavenly Father.

This principle of free substitution most manifestly pervades, or rather, more correctly speaking, is in its very self the essence of the great prime cardinal operation of the gospel, namely justification.

The two component parts of justification which are pardon of sin and imputation of righteousness are each of course an absolutely free gift. Both are given of free grace, and both exist only through the operation of the principle of substitution.

They are the results of our substitute's sacrifice and sufferings, the purchase and fruits of His merits and obedience.

With regard to the pardon of sin, it is so manifestly the doctrine of Scripture, so clearly expressed and so imperatively demanded throughout the whole scope of Bible teaching, with reference to the satisfaction requisite for sin, that it is obtainable solely as the result of and only on account of the one great sacrifice, that even error itself may furnish evidence, if needs were, to this effect and midst the many false views which have been, and are, entertained with regard to the necessity for seeking the preparation of some personal fitness as a necessary condition precedent to the participation in the benefits of pardon, perhaps by far the most commonly prevailing form of error may be accepted as that which professes, in all the spurious humility of self-righteous though perhaps undreamt of pride, rather to endeavour after some personal befitment for the enjoyment of that which has been confessedly so dearly, and undoubtedly already long since bought by another, than with presumptuous audacity to openly attempt to share in its purchase.

There is present under such circumstances a deeply rooted and influencing conviction, that however the personal endeavours of the suppliant may be requisite to move God to pitifully and mercifully bestow a right to its enjoyment, the original purchase is itself a thing that man 'must leave alone for ever, for it cost more to redeem his soul.'

Of course the idea of any preparatory fitness, save that of necessity, being required as a title to the acceptance of the gospel is erroneous and sinful, but there, even in the midst of misapprehension or denial of God's word, may be found a tacit testimony to the substitutionary character of the atoning sacrifice.

But better far to cite the very words of Scripture than appeal to any indirect corroboration, however manifest or striking.

Take that familiar chapter in Isaiah, the overheard perusal of a portion of which afforded the Evangelist an opportunity for preaching Jesus to the Ethiopian treasurer, where it is written, 'He was wounded for our transgressions, He was bruised for our iniquities' (Isa. liii. 3).

Shall we listen to the testimony of John the Baptist when in Bethabara beyond Jordan he saw Jesus approaching and said, 'Behold the Lamb of God which taketh away (beareth) the sin of the world' (John i. 29)?

Shall we take the very words of Christ Himself at that strangely solemn interview, when, in the stillness of night, the mysteries of the kingdom were expounded to the wondering Nicodemus, and the grand old historic picture of the arid wilderness, and the viper-stung Israelites, and the brazen serpent was recalled to mind to point to the then present antitype, 'For God so loved the world that He gave His only-begotten Son' (John iii. 16)?

Or shall we visit the upper chamber, when just before going forth to dark Gethsemane, at the institution of the memorial feast, our Blessed Saviour said, 'This is my blood of the new testament which is shed for many for the remission of sins' (Matt. xxvi. 28)?

In that Epistle which is, so to speak, pre-eminently devoted to the enunciation of justification through faith we find, 'Whom (Christ Jesus) God hath set forth to be a propitiation through faith in His blood' (Rom. iii. 25).

'He was delivered for our offences' (Rom. iv. 25).

'Christ died for the ungodly' (Rom. v. 6).

'While we were yet sinners Christ died for us' (Rom. v. 8).

'God sending His own Son in the likeness of sinful flesh and for sin (by a sacrifice for sin) condemned sin in the flesh' (Rom. viii. 3).

'He that spared not His own Son, but delivered Him up for us all' (Rom. viii. 32).

Equally abundant in specific reference to the reality of substitution is the Epistle to the Hebrews.

There, amidst the abounding allusion to the services and sacrifices of the tabernacle and temple, are to be found of necessity testimonies to the substitutionary character of that one great for ever complete offering of which all these were but types and shadows: 'He hath appeared to put away sin by the sacrifice of Himself' (Heb. ix. 26).

'Christ was once offered to bear the sins of many' (Heb. ix. 28).

'Neither by the blood of goats and calves but by His own blood He entered in once into the holy place, having obtained eternal redemption for us. For if the blood of bulls and of goats and the ashes of an heifer sprinkling the unclean sanctifieth to the purifying of the flesh, how much more shall the blood of Christ' (Heb. ix. 12, 13).

'By the which will we are sanctified through

the offering of the blood of Jesus Christ once for all' (Heb. x. 10).

'Jesus, that He might sanctify the people with His own blood, suffered without the gate' (Heb. xiii. 12).

In the First Epistle of Peter we read: 'Forasmuch as ye know that ye were not redeemed with corruptible things, but with the precious blood of Christ' (1 Pet. i. 18, 19).

'His own self bear our own sin in His own body on the tree' (1 Pet. ii. 24).

'Christ hath once suffered for sins the just for the unjust' (1 Pet. iii. 18).

'Christ hath once suffered for us in the flesh' (1 Pet. iv. 1).

The Christians at Corinth are told: 'Christ died for our sins' (1 Cor. xv. 3).

'He died for all' (2 Cor. v. 15).

The Colossians are addressed: 'And you hath He reconciled in the body of His flesh through death' (Col. i. 22, 23).

Such quotations may surely suffice, nor will further testimony be here adduced, save the declaration of the beloved disciple: 'He is the propitiation for our sins: and not for ours only, but also for the sins of the whole world' (1 John ii. 2).

If the teaching of Scripture is thus clear, explicit, and absolute with regard to the way in which satisfaction for sin has been made, it is no less so in reference to the origin and nature of that perfect righteousness in which the believer must be arrayed, and perpetually clad, in order to be and appear justified in the sight of God.

It too is the work of Another. It too is the work of Christ. It is not partly of ourselves, as pardoned sinners, and partly of Christ as a helper in our salvation, but solely and entirely of Christ. It is as much and truly so as the propitiatory sacrifice. There is moreover no other righteousness which can avail us in the sight of God.

We have this or we have none.

It is only in respect of this righteousness, the result of Christ's obedience imputed to us and received through faith, that we can be just in the sight of God or live the life of the just.

Before proceeding to the selection of passages from the New Testament Scriptures, attention may be well directed to two or three references in the pages of the Old.

This course may all the more advantageously be pursued, since from the little prominence given to it, more truly speaking the almost utter absence of even the barest mention of it, by certain schools of modern theology, this doctrine of *imputed* righteousness may be thought of by some, perhaps many, as almost a strange novelty in doctrine or unpractical and unnecessary refinement of an over-strained metaphysical scholastic divinity.

That it is not either, any more than it was a principle of the life of faith operating for the first time in the early Christian Church, and in consequence of apostolic teachings, is proved by the words of St. Paul; for, though he speaks of it as 'now manifested,' he also describes it as 'witnessed by the law and the prophets.'

So that, though undoubtedly it was reserved till after the 'fulness of the time' to be set forth 'that he who runs may read,' it had in prophetic days been, as part of the great principle of justification by faith, the hope of righteousness to the true worshipper of old.

Take then those passages in the Psalms:

'Blessed are they whose iniquities are forgiven, and whose sins are covered;

'Blessed is the man to whom the Lord will not impute sin' (Ps. xxxii. 1).

'I will make mention of Thy righteousness, even of Thine only' (Ps. lxxi. 16).

'Thou shalt answer for me, O God.'

'Blessed is the people that know the joyful sound: they shall walk, O Lord, in the light of Thy countenance.

'In Thy name shall they rejoice all the day: and in Thy righteousness shall they be exalted' (Ps. lxxxix. 15 and 16).

The testimony of the prophet Isaiah to the imputed nature of the believer's justifying righteousness, when showing of the glorious privileges, recompensing comforts, sure defence, and royal heritage of the redeemed servants, is:

'Their righteousness is of me, saith the Lord' (Isa. liv. 17).

Jeremiah, when foretelling the reign of the promised Messiah, the raising 'unto David a righteous branch, and a king' that should 'reign and prosper and execute judgment and justice in the earth,' goes on to say:

'In his days Judah shall be saved, and Israel shall dwell safely, and this is his name whereby he

G

shall be called, the Lord our Righteousness' (Jer. xxiii. 6).

Passing now to a review of New Testament declarations as to this wondrous and, be it ever borne in mind, indispensable gift.

In the Epistle to the Romans we find the great Apostle of the Gentiles saying:

'For I am not ashamed of the gospel of Christ: for it is the power of God unto salvation to every one that believeth;

'For therein is the righteousness of God revealed from faith to faith: as it is written, The just shall live by faith' (Rom. i. 16, 17).

'By the deeds of the law there shall no flesh be justified in his sight: for by the law is the knowledge of sin.

'But now the righteousness of God without the law is manifested, being witnessed by the law and the prophets;

'Even the righteousness of God which is by faith of Jesus Christ unto all and upon all them that believe' (Rom. iii. 20, 21, 22).

'To him that worketh not, but believeth on him that justifieth the ungodly, his faith is counted for righteousness.

'Even as David also describeth the blessedness of the man to whom God imputeth righteousness without works' (Rom. iv. 5, 6).

Referring to the example of Abraham, 'strong in faith, giving glory to God;' 'fully persuaded that what He had promised, He was able also to perform,' he goes on to say:

'It was imputed to him for righteousness.'

'Now it was not written for his sake alone, that it was imputed to him;

'But for us also, to whom it shall be imputed, if we believe on Him that raised up Jesus our Lord from the dead' (Rom. iv. 22, 23, 24).

Again we find:

'For if by one man's offence death reigned by one; much more they which receive abundance of grace and of the gift of righteousness shall reign in life by one, Jesus Christ. Therefore as by the offence of one (Adam) judgment came upon all men to condemnation; even so by the righteousness of one the free gift came upon all men unto justification of life.

'For as by one man's disobedience many were made sinners, so by the obedience of one shall many be made righteous' (Rom. v. 17, 18, 19).

'What shall we say then? That the Gentiles, which followed not after righteousness, have attained to righteousness, even the righteousness which is of faith.

'But Israel, which followed after the law of righteousness, hath not attained to the law of righteousness. Wherefore? Because they sought it not by faith, but as it were by the works of the law' (Rom. ix. 30, 31, 32).

And then, by and by, we come to that magnificent outburst of most ennobled patriotism, intensified and sanctified by that burning and devoted love which permeated and inspired the heart's life of the devoted writer, so enthusiastic a regard for his countrymen as could elsewhere break forth in expressions of readiness to be himself accursed if they might thereby live.

'Brethren, my heart's desire and prayer to God for Israel is that they might be saved.

'For I bear them record that they have a zeal of God, but not according to knowledge.

'For they, being ignorant of God's righteousness, and going about to establish their own righteousness, have not submitted themselves to the righteousness of God.

'For Christ is the end of the law for righteousness to every one that believeth' (Rom. x. 1, 2, 3, 4).

The Corinthian Church are told:

'Of Him are ye in Christ Jesus, who of God is made unto us wisdom and righteousness, and sanctification, and redemption' (1 Cor. i. 30).

The Galatians have the solemn truth brought before them in few but how meaning words:

'If righteousness come by the law, then Christ is dead in vain' (Gal. ii. 21).

The great tragedy of Calvary worthless, and of no avail!

No wonder that one who knew that this was so, who felt in all its overpowering force, its full appalling significance, as a stern and unconquerable reality, as indeed the very truth, should, after the summing up of all that had gone to form a religious life, strict, praiseworthy, faultless, hardly approached by the ordinary mortal, willingly and gladly renounce and trample upon all, that stript of every figment of human make he might be able to say:

'And be found in Him, not having mine own righteousness, which is of the law, but that which is through the faith of Christ, the righteousness which is of God by faith' (Phil. iii. 9).

Now these passages, above quoted, prove conclusively and clearly that pardon has been bought, and a justifying righteousness long since wrought out, each as truly and as perfectly as the other, through the finished substitutionary work of our Lord and Saviour.

As a consequence the one may be as fully treated as a reality as the other, and, supposing that either could be used apart from the other, it might be so employed with equal justice, and equal certainty of its efficacy.

But seeing that they together form the ground of that justification through faith which is the only justification in the sight of God, and that so they cannot be separated in their action, or as gifts be accepted and enjoyed apart from one another, neither ought they to be so treated in Christian teaching as if they were.

The inculcation of the acceptance of and dependence on the one is as much demanded, in the true preaching of the gospel, as the acceptance of and dependence on the other, for they together make up the substitutionary work of our Lord and Saviour.

It is as true 'that Christ is the end of the law

for righteousness to every one that believeth,' as that 'He is the propitiation for our sins.'

To withhold the setting forth of the former, whilst announcing the latter, is to present an imperfect gospel, and so to practically misrepresent what God has done for man.

To tell of pardon without telling also of the imputed righteousness, which is its accompaniment, is to preach but part of the gospel; and where that is done there need be little, or rather no wonder, if there be uncertain peace and little if any real joy, and results altogether very different to those which followed that complete declaration of the truth as it is in Jesus, which proved the really good news of apostolic days.

The withholding of the announcement of the entire fulfilment of the law (as a means of justifying righteousness in the sight of God) on behalf of and for every believer, the most feeble as well as the strongest in faith, is a withholding of essential gospel truth, and a bearing false witness to the work of Christ. Glory be to God, 'though we believe not yet He remaineth faithful, He cannot deny Himself;' and when the sinner has obtained pardon and acceptance as a believer he has also obtained the imputed righteousness which is attained through faith. But then, like the heir of rich inheritance, toiling in ignorance of his wealth in a foreign land, in reality rich but practically needy, the helpless possessor of mighty power, he who is treading with heavy, because uncertain, heart the weary path of a semi-emancipated life, the possessor of privileges as a means of comfort and encouragement and strength, unenjoyed because unknown, is manifestly not in that condition of existence where we could naturally or reasonably expect that bright and cheerful obedience which is only to be found where and when the knowledge of the truth has made free.

If there be any advantage whatever to be anticipated from the training up of children 'in the way in which they should go,' surely such advantage must be proportionate to the acquaintance with, and regard to, the nature of the way which is manifested and turned to account by those who profess to direct them.

The way is the way of holiness to the Lord. None can enter upon that way but the justified. None can traverse it with altogether willing and ready feet, and perfectly peaceful, not to say absolutely joyous, heart, but such as has not only heard of and laved in the fountain opened for sin and for uncleanness, but is also consciously clad in the consecrated and all-covering robes of the Redeemer's righteousness.

CHAPTER VIII.

SURROUNDINGS.

THERE may be some, possibly not a few, who whilst quite ready to accept to the full the testimony of Scripture as to the natural and inherent depravity and impotency for good of each individual, and equally willing to admit the absolute necessity of the regenerating and sanctifying power of the Holy Ghost, are not so apt to acknowledge and recognize, or at all events sufficiently appreciate, the forces of antagonism and hindrance to the application and enjoyment of the gospel remedy, in its various stages, which are presented by the circumstances of human life.

And yet the moral atmosphere amidst which the gospel is to be taught, accepted, and obeyed, has much to do with creating and increasing the difficulties of the life of faith.

The surroundings, even in the most favoured of lots, are not altogether friendly, whilst in the majority, perhaps even in the ordinary run, of cases they are most undeniably, as they are very often manifestly, opposed and more or less inimical to spiritual health and progress. The work of instruction in the truth as it is in Jesus is to be undertaken, and carried on in the midst of many difficulties and in the face of many and powerful foes.

In addition to the resistance from within, springing from that natural and inherent depravity to which reference has been already so fully made, there are the various external hindrances on the part of human fellow-creatures, either as individuals or as members of confederations, domestic, social, political, or religious.

These, whether assuming the character of active incentives to or direct encouragements in evil, or confined to the less ostentatious but not necessarily less effective influences of tacit suggestion and bad example, are of fearful efficacy either to confirm the wrong or undermine the right.

Nor ought there to be overlooked the pernicious effects of bad example on the part of those who, although restrained by the blessed power of heavenly grace from contaminating their fellows by the wilful, greedy, and undisguised pursuit of the pleasures of profligacy and sin, through the inconsistency of their behaviour whilst professing children of light ofttimes grievously hinder and harm the cause they at heart truly love.

These the well-known, and more or less clearly apparent, are not all the difficulties that obstruct, or the only foes that assail. There is the fearful opposition of the malignant personal powers of spiritual darkness, with their beguiling, ensnaring, perplexing, and deceiving suggestions, and their malicious designs, backed by superhuman influence and power.

All these together go to form an aggregate of circumstances, which nothing but the miracle-working power of the Deity can successfully combat and vanquish.

It should be hardly necessary to adduce quotations from Scripture for the purpose of describing the moral atmosphere or delineating the character of this present evil world, or to show how opposed the motives, desires, and developments of thought, not only in regard to material interests but in relation to the unseen, whenever cognizance is taken of its existence, which actuate and characterize its policy, and bear sway over the domain of intellect and heart and soul, are to the mind and will of God as declared in the Bible.

The spirit of the Bible so testifies to the opposition of the spirit of the world to the kingdom of heaven, that it should seem impossible to rise from a candid, though even very superficial, perusal of the inspired Word, without the conviction that there exists an absolutely irreconcilable difference, or rather an implacable animosity, between the spirit of the world and the spirit of the gospel. The world is ever looked upon, and referred to, as not only unfriendly but altogether actively antagonistic to the Christian's welfare. This is not of course to say that it is impossible that the enjoyment of an overflowing meed of temporal prosperity should, in modern as in patriarchal days, when the heaven-determined lot of any special believer, serve to testify that, now as then, godliness hath the promise of this life as well as of that which is to come; or even to wish to appear to deny that in the faithful use of the advantages and opportunities afforded by the enjoyment of love-empowering affluence the gracious and all-swaying influence of the Divine Spirit may not be, or often is, rendered more conspicuously prominent.

Wealth may be employed aright. This world, in the sense of material advantages and prosperity, when such fall to the lot of the believer, is to be pressed into the service of Him who is its rightful Lord. 'The Father of all mercies.' 'The Giver of every good and every perfect gift,' 'whose is the silver and the gold.'

The enjoined duty of the Christian is to use this world 'as not abusing it,' and the sanctified possession of wealth, power, and their attendant influences, though accompanied with a fearfully enlarged responsibility, gives at the same time immensely increased potentialities for glorifying God through and in the display of love to man.

Wealth may be, in truth frequently is, employed aright. The rules, however, which govern such employment and use are as little of the world as the spirit and frame of mind which prompts obedience to them. They are not the outcome of that 'wisdom of the world' which 'is foolishness with God.'

What is in Scripture for moral and spiritual

purposes designated as the world, is manifestly not so much that realm of nature, the mantling garb of the material globe, with its glorious panoramas of peak, and wood, and ocean, rich plains, broad streams, sweet vales, and placid lakes.

Nor so much, unless it be by implication when they are referred to as the enlisted or enslaved allies of sin and evil, the various heaven-ordained and necessary adjuncts, and in their natures innocent requirements, of our corporeal mundane existence.

The term 'world' would seem rather to refer, if not explicitly to be attached, to that domain of the lust of the flesh, of the lust of the eye, and of the pride of life, which together embrace all that is in that invisible but ever busy realm of mind, and motive, and aim, the course of which is according to the behests of 'the prince of the power of the air, the spirit that now worketh in the children of disobedience.'

And just as the kingdom of God is invisible and internal, so do these hold unseen court within the human breast, and rule, and reign, and show their presence by the overt life.

The term 'world,' save when manifestly referring

to the work of material creation, serves in Scripture to denominate an atmosphere of thought, taste, aim, purpose, and pursuit, not only uncongenial and unfavourable, but absolutely noxious to the spiritual life, animated in policy and characterized in action by principles and aims diametrically opposed to the dogmas and maxims of gospel teaching, and of course, as a necessary consequence, at total and absolute variance in aim and object with the life of faith.

Now the evil influence and blasting presence of the world, as thus understood, extend far beyond the region of the openly and admittedly flagitious and immoral.

This very world has its code of morality, and in some respects the compliance with its outward demands closely approximates, and in other absolutely agrees with, the external ethics of Christianity.

To the eye of the average observer, that behaviour and course of action which may win the plaudits of the approving or admiring multitude, whether on account of the manifest natural and essential justice by which it is characterized, or by reason of the directly resulting practical benefits which seem likely to accrue therefrom, is to all appearance similar whether met with in the conduct of a declared and approved believer or of a professing infidel.

And yet there is a difference, and that a most fundamental one. In the one case it is the outcome and fruit of faith; in the other it is, however beneficial to mankind, absolutely sin, for 'whatsoever is not of faith is sin.'

In the midst of our modern civilization, manifestly affected as it has so long been by the more or less direct influence of the gospel, if it is not in truth in every predominant and distinctive feature absolutely the result of its presence and teachings, it is perhaps not unfrequently next to, if not absolutely, impossible, and that none the less so owing to the necessary similarity in operation which pervades all such works, to know whether to regard full many a highly vaunted and eulogized philanthropic undertaking as justly entitled to honour as a work of Christian love.

Pretensions of nomenclature in the cases of public institutions are not, any more than reputations for sanctity in those of private individuals or corporate bodies, either always, or altogether, reliable guarantees as to true character, and the principles on which, no less than the modes in which, much undeniable practical benevolence may be applied, whether for relief of pecuniary distress, or the alleviation of physical suffering, or the promotion of social welfare, or the ensuring of domestic comfort, may be after all but outcomes and developments of some form or other of lust or pride.

Even mere worldly policy may suggest the advisability of a kind and liberal consideration for the wants of the poor and needy; for that spurious philanthropy which takes its rise either in the love of gratitude or of applause, or perhaps springs in truth from a judicious dread of future violence or reprisal, is after all but a sordid outcome and development of pure selfishness.

Indeed, as has been very well suggested by a modern philosopher, much that is referred to as admirable, and lovable, in the behaviour of mankind may really, after all, be but the operation of blind and irresistible impulse or instinct; and when traced to its true source, even the maternal love which would perish of exposure in the wintry blast, to save the helpless babe, may be found wondrously akin to that fond attachment of the beast of prey which would urge the tigress upon certain destruction, to seek the safety of her little cubs.

Then, too, there may be that practical tribute to the efficacy and advantage of virtue that can and may, though perhaps at the cost of considerable self-sacrifice, adopt the insignia of the Christian graces. The practice of the great temporally advantageous principles of truth in business transactions, honesty in dealings, purity in overt act, and the discharge generally of the kindly and endearing offices of friendship, may be, as bringing each its own immediate and tangible reward, very well often accepted as rules of conduct by even the most worldly-minded of mankind.

Lines of conduct apparently similar to those which should characterize believers in the Gospel are thus to be seen pursued, and that by no means unfrequently, in relation to the practice of those virtues which are susceptible in exercise of ostentatious display.

From one cause or another even the gospel virtues of love to enemies, kindness to the ungrateful, the returning of good for evil, and even the practice of painful self-denial for the sake of others, may at times be, very doubtless not unfrequently are, present in effective and beneficent operation in the behaviour of avowed sceptics of the only way of salvation.

Nor is it to be denied that these coincidences with the manifested results of the acceptance of the Gospel ofttimes partake of the character of devotion, and are in fact the religious exercises of an unscriptural system of will-worship, the display of an earth-born and world-constructed religion, perhaps as worthless and displeasing in the sight of heaven as the hideous rites of heathendom, though practised in the midst of a nominally Christian civilization.

The morality of utility or of self-righteousness, credentialed as it may be by the wisdom of experience, and approved as it may be by the dictates of mundane sagacity, and coinciding as it may in external particulars with the morality of the gospel, is still, as the offspring of unbelief and the foster child of pride, inimical to the true interests of the human race; and the light which it can throw upon the path of life is at best but much akin to the delusive meteor of the pestilential marsh, or the wrecker's fire upon the rock-bound shore.

Nor is it in the fields of secular enterprise alone that there is danger. These same factors of evil, the lust of the flesh, and the lust of the eye, and the pride of life, are to be found even within the consecrated precincts of the very sanctuary of the Most High, and are ever and anon declaring their presence in the hearts of the very redeemed, and though there crushed and kept under by restraining grace are ever ready and liable, at any moment, to assert their powers.

And if the hearts of the faithful are not proof against the machinations of lust and pride, is it any wonder if in that great cosmopolitan congregation of worshippers, the visible Church, where true believer and mere professing formalist not only unite their voices in the ritual of prayer and praise, but conjoin in labours to direct and rule, can it be any wonder if there those subtile influences which can distract, and harass, and distress the sacred quiet of the hour of lonely prayer, should ofttimes revel and run riot amid the bitterness of controversy, and the frenzy of hot debate, or beckon on with fiendish delight in the mad blind race of wild ambition?

Even, busy with the development of the most

single-minded and devoted enterprises for the glory of God and the good of their fellow-men, true and leal-hearted servants of the King of kings must needs be on their guard lest the very devotion of burning zeal should afford cover for the stealthy advances of envy, jealousy, and hate. The very gifts of inanimate nature, the beauteous scene, the balmy air, the exhilarating atmosphere, the rich abundance of the material world, that should at least, it might have been thought, have remained inactive spectators of the awful strife of the heart's rebellion, are, alas! too often enlisted in the cause of evil, so that often it appears too sadly and unmistakeably manifest that 'the things which should have been for' men's 'good' become literally to them 'an occasion of falling.'

There are indeed two, and only two, sides, on one or the other of which man and his belongings must be found ranged. Man cannot serve God and mammon. And as with man, so also with all the influences of his surroundings. They too are enlisted on the one side or the other. According as the motive which inspires to its employment, so is the thing employed sanctified or desecrated in its use.

Till the motive is itself consecrated, all without and around is, if not actively, at least potentially, mischievous.

Against the service of sin, the world, and the devil, formally at the baptismal font, actually when indeed baptized by the regenerating, and consecrating, and sanctifying power of the Holy Spirit, the Christian is enlisted, and the combined ceaseless enmity and opposition of these three is the condition of lifelong existence.

CHAPTER IX.

APPLICATION.

HAVING established on the sure basis of the Divine testimony, the true natural properties, tendencies, and capabilities of man; having ascertained from the same source the ultimate and supreme object of all human existence, and so determined the great end to which all upbringing should be directed and subordinate; having briefly considered the gospel, through the reception and application of which in its simplicity and fulness this end of man's being can alone be accomplished in safety and peace; and having adverted to the nature of the surroundings and moral atmosphere amidst which this gospel is to be taught, accepted, and obeyed, we would now proceed to the consideration of the mode in which its beneficent provisions are to be applied to the young, so as to endeavour to ensure, in a system of upbringing which is the embodiment of those principles of procedure through which such application can alone be brought about, the attaining so far as may be of all the varied benefits for time, as well as for eternity, which result from obedience to the doctrines of the cross.

Now it is to be accepted as a fundamental principle, in attempting to provide for this application, that the temporal advantages are to be treated as consequent on, and in truth looked for only as resultant from, the possession of the eternal benefits, and that the advantages which accrue to the believer with reference to the present life ensue directly from, and are the absolute outcomes of the training for the enjoyment of a future existence.

It need, moreover, hardly be necessary to point out that by temporal need not by any means be necessarily implied material advantages in the grosser sense of wealth, power, and their concomitant gratifications of appetite, sense, and sight, but rather the intangible though not less real pleasures of peace, happiness, and joy.

The former may or may not be the accompaniments of the latter, but they are not objects to be pre-eminently sought after, or even desired at all, save in consonance with the revealed will of God, and subserviently to His glory. An all-merciful and all-bountiful Creator has indeed so ruled the order of sequences, in the matter of material providence, that obedience to His will, in providing for eternity, does, by reflex influence upon the behaviour in reference to the conduct and affairs of this present life, serve to supply, and that frequently in no meagre or stinted dole, the necessities and even superfluities of the earthly sojourn.

The Almighty has even pledged His providence to provide for the indispensable temporal requirements of His children: 'Thy bread shall be given thee, thy water shall be sure.' But beyond such assurance, there is no absolute connection of the good things of this life with the better things of the future, and external prosperity, as understood in the expression 'worldly success,' is not to be calculated on as a necessary accompaniment of a believing life, much less is it to be adopted as an object to be pre-eminently striven for, or even ardently desired, save with a view to the glory of God. Still less should it be sought after, or provision sedulously made for the attainment of its possession, in ways which either clearly contravene or openly contemn the behests of the Most High.

It is perfectly true that the active exercises of those virtues of honesty, integrity, sobriety, and diligence, which are enjoined as part of the loving service of the redeemed, are the very means in the ordinary course of events, common to all, calculated to ensure what is popularly known as 'success in life,' and equally true that they generally lead to its attainment, in greater or lesser degree; but they are to be exercised, irrespectively of any regard to temporal results, as part of that great sacrifice of obedience, which is the life business of the believer, and which may, or may not, be acknowledged and rewarded according to human ideas in part in the present portion of existence, as may seem good to our Heavenly Father.

When the words, 'Seek ye first the kingdom of God and His righteousness,' fell from the lips of our adorable Redeemer, as around and far beneath across the spreading slopes of the Galilean hill the great and wondering multitude listened in rapt attention to Him who 'spake as never man spake,' an authoritative enunciation was therein given of the great ruling principle which should ever govern the conduct of human life. They indicate that order of action, and that line of behaviour, which, if never as then so precisely determined and enjoined, must, with knowledge of the true relative importance of the spiritual compared with the corporeal interests of humanity, such as every even nominal Christian may be fairly assumed to possess, from the mere fact of his religious profession, manifestly appear the truly wise and only rational. Attention to such a statement might even be expected were it to be regarded merely as a commonplace hypothesis of far-sighted prudence, and placed on an equality with many another, the truth of which as supported by experience, or the probable utility of which as estimated by careful and sound judgment, has elevated to the rank of a dictum of sound philosophy. But in this injunction we hear not the words of mere human wisdom, however intrinsically sound or how much soever supported by the evidence of experience, or prompted by the most penetrating created sagacity, but the voice of heavenly wisdom from the lips of Very God Incarnate. Now if this is to be accepted, as it most certainly is, as the infallible rule for the grown-up human being, and the object of upbringing, described in the most general terms, must on all hands be equally readily admitted to be the befitting of youth for the discharge of the duties and responsibilities of maturer years, and for the best and most advantageous use and employment of life and its opportunities, it necessarily follows that attention to the requirements of this rule ought to be paid most especially in the conduct of the upbringing of the young. The recognition of such necessity, whencesoever its knowledge may have been derived, whether it might be from the consideration of these identical words of our Lord to which reference has just been made, or from one or other of the many passages of Scripture of similar import, or even in some, perhaps many, cases immediately through the medium of personal observation and experience, has obtained for religious instruction that place to which it is presumably entitled, and which it does *ostensibly* hold in all professedly Christian upbringing. It is not that there is, or indeed could possibly be, any admitted doubt in the minds of professing Christians as to the fundamental place which specific religious training ought to occupy in the upbringing of the young. How could there be? Some appreciation of the value of religious training may be found amongst those who do not even profess themselves believers in the gospel for their personal salvation. There are those who, deeming themselves too secure in their native virtue, and too correct in their demeanour, to require any of those adventitious aids which are requisite for those of dimmer intelligence, and weaker will, and halting moral gait, are not only willing to admit the value, but ready enough to urge the necessity, of some sort of religious training, as a department of social police. There may be those, too, sunk in almost hopeless despondency, if not well-nigh blank despair, because though desirous of peace and joy, not yet thoroughly acquainted with the true and only source of all comfort, who would fain, by inculcating the advantages of possessing a mind early imbued with Divine truth, and directed by higher than human wisdom, strive to secure for others in early youth that aid and vantage-ground the lack of which they themselves so keenly deplore. Such, whilst not yet acquainted with the gospel in all its fulness, are yet sufficiently enlightened to see that it is in the implanting of the germs of religion, and in that alone, there is to be sought the panacea for all earthly needs and guidance furnished for the voyage of life. Even these various classes concur with believers in acknowledging the propriety of a religious upbringing. But religious is not of necessity Christian. And nominally Christian is not always strictly or truly gospel. Would that it were, in the best interests of humanity at large, and more especially of the young! Overlaid by vain traditions, fettered by worldly surroundings, maligned by the evil within, traduced by the evil without, obscured by false teaching, perverted, misrepresented, and distorted, the gospel, true, full, free, and untrammelled, is often, if not actually absent, at least hardly to be distinguished in the doctrine and practice of many in the visible church. If such be the fact as regards parent and teacher, can it be any wonder that the best interests of the child and pupil should suffer?

Bound to admit the fundamental place which religious training should occupy in the upbringing of the young, professing Christians may however doubt as to whether in the quiet seclusion of home, or in the busy whirl of the public class-room, the child can with more advantage be made acquainted with the things appertaining to his or her eternal peace, but never for a moment would they demur to professed acquiescence with, and eager enforcement of the injunction, to 'train up a child in the way in which he should go.'

To judge, however, from the variety of action displayed in the professed reduction to practice of that injunction, there would appear to be some very decided and marked differences of opinion with regard to what is now involved in obeying it. All turns upon what is to be accepted as the way. That in turn will be decided by the degree of appreciation of the truth of the gospel, which may happen to be enjoyed by the parent or preceptor. That the saying of the wise old Hebrew monarch has been in modern times, and in the full light of the Christian dispensation, followed to the full in its necessarily altered application to the changed circumstances of those born under the gospel economy, and that with manifest success, ought not to be for one moment doubted. That it has also in the course of the Christian centuries been conscientiously striven, and honestly assumed, to have been carried out by far more, whilst from lack of knowledge they themselves have not been possessed of such acquaintance with those resources of the gospel in its entirety which were absolutely necessary to the attaining of the object so dear to their heart, is also a matter about which there can be little reasonable doubt.

There moreover not only have been, but undoubtedly are, those who professing to be thoroughly intimate with the details of the gospel salvation, though looking upon it as absolutely fitted for the full grown, have doubted, and still doubt, the propriety, or expediency, or safety, of disclosing its free and gracious benefits in all their fulness to the youthful mind. Nor is there any wonder that this should be so, for such are but following the example of many professedly evangelical teachers who regard with similar dread the proclaiming the plain teaching of the great Apostle of the Gentiles.

It all turns upon what is to be accepted as the way. That way has in all ages been determined and fixed by God, and for us it is in the obeying of the gospel of Christ.

For the child of the Israelite, born and bred in the land of promise, the instruction in the way of God's righteousness was ordained to be through the intervention and medium of the law moral and ceremonial, for the child of the Christian it is to be direct through the displaying and imparting of the knowledge of the gospel and law of grace.

The Hebrew child was instructed and trained up in the observance of the elaborate sacrificial and ceremonial ritual of the Mosaic dispensation, a dispensation which moreover imparted through the promulgation of its ordained and sanctioned jurisprudence a religious character to the meanest transaction of everyday life. The child of the Christian is to be reared in the knowledge of the one great sacrifice, propitiation, and satisfaction, and subsequently to be familiarized with all the details of behaviour consistent therewith, in religious, political, social, and domestic life, which ought to accompany, follow, evidence, and characterize the actual and participating interest in, and possession of, its varied and manifold purchased blessings.

That religious upbringing in short, which not only befits, but is the bounden duty of the professing Christian, unless determined to disregard alike the teaching of Scripture and the dictates of enlightened common sense, is not, and cannot be, that mere familiarizing the infant or juvenile mind with Scripture biography, or that acquiring by memory of the precise verbal phraseology of the sacred text, or that learning by rote of the decalogue, or that lecturing upon the propriety and advantage of the exercise of the little virtues of childhood, or that prompting to any or all of those vague and indefinite attempts to propitiate the Deity by dutiful behaviour, which seem regarded by some as the indispensable preparation of the juvenile mind for the inculcation at some future day of the knowledge of the gospel.

How universally employed, and how generally passing current, as ample and sufficient, not only for infants of tender years, but for children of well-developed faculties, and in ordinary matters treated as of sharp understandings and ready parts, may be left to the judgment and conscience of the reader.

It must be teaching of a very different sort that is justly entitled to the appellation of gospel teaching.

It just comes to this, the object of gospel teaching must be the subjects-matter of the gospel, and if the very nature of the gospel demands that a certain order is to be observed in the teaching of those subjects, then such order must be followed in their application to the case of any.

Now the gospel is immutable. It is ever and always the same. There is not one gospel for the youthful sinner, and another for the hoary-headed reprobate. Its proffered remedy is ever the same, just as the requirements of every child of Adam, for its saving influence and sovereign power, are in every case essentially alike, virtually the same. Varied as may be the distinguishing characteristic needs, and special transgressions, of each of the multitude of cases to which it may be applied, in every instance with equal propriety, and ever with the like certainty of success, the great facts and superhuman operations on which its efficacy and power depend, and through which its application and employment alike for justification and sanctification is effected, are of necessity in each case absolutely similar, identically the same.

In each instance it is sin, hereditary and actual, which has to be atoned for, covered, subdued, and eradicated, and such atonement is ever the same in each case, that once and for ever made for the sins of the whole world on Calvary, such covering is effected in every case by the same imputation of the same righteousness, long since wrought out by the one sole Saviour and representative, and that subjugation and eradication of evil, however varied in the rapidity of its achievement, is ever the work of the same Holy Spirit, as the purchased consequence of the same one great work.

And just as there is need for the application of all the benefits of the redemption for one grown-up sinner as for another, so does there exist equal need for the same gospel, in the like completeness for the youngest, as for the oldest, intelligent human being. Differences of age are just of as little moment as differences in social position, intellectual culture, or respectability in the eyes of the world, in affecting the needs of their possessors for the same Saviour and the same salvation. With regard to the applicability of the facts, and principles and provisions of the gospel to the needs and requirements of the adult, no question could for a moment arise in the mind of any who held the faith in its primitive, and absolutely unchangeable simplicity.

Nay further, not only could no such question arise as to their applicability, but to demur to the absolute necessity of their acceptance and belief in order to his or her salvation would be to reject, as by necessary implication, the gospel remedy.

To deny man's natural depravity, consequent upon his fall in the person of his first representative, would be to deny the truth of that scriptural estimate of man's true natural character, and impotency to satisfy the requirements of a life devoted to the willing and accepted service of God, which underlies the whole system of salvation through Christ. To demur, no matter on what grounds, to the sole justifying efficacy of that righteousness which is the free gift of God, and which is so far as the recipient is concerned the acceptance of an absolute discharge from all the requirements of the law as a means of justification in God's sight, would be a denial, though possibly at first sight it might not so appear,—a virtual rejection of the work of our blessed Saviour, effecting as that did not only a satisfaction for the punishment due to every active infraction of the Divine law, but supplying moreover that perfect and meritorious obedience to every particular of its varied enactments which the requirements of inexorable justice must exact, as indispensably necessary to the discharge of a perfect obedience.

Many who would shudder at the mere suggestion of their being thought capable of calling in question the truth of Scripture in reference to the depravity of human nature, or of impugning the full sufficiency of the atoning sacrifice, practically seem to ignore both by withholding from their children thorough instruction, at the earliest possible opportunity, in the doctrine of justification by faith.

Such parents or preceptors practically, whatever may be their intentions with regard to the future, for the time being substitute law for gospel. They do that which, as contrary to the revealed will of God, can at no time be defended as the correct course, however it may recommend itself on grounds of fleshly wisdom, and they do so at that very period of life when credence comes so to speak, if not actually, instinctively, with the heart, such as it is, most impressionable; with the will most plastic; and ere the fascinations of unlawful pleasure and the tyranny of evil habit have acquired much, if any, control; at that very period, in short, when the most favourable of opportunities is afforded for sowing the seed of life.

It seems scarcely comprehensible that any who know that the key to their own spiritual safety and prosperity was the knowledge of the gospel, and who are aware of the truth with regard to the relationship of the gospel to the law, and are cognizant of the solemn warnings of the New Testament and of the fearful responsibilities of rejecting or scouting the offers, so absolutely necessary as they moreover must know them to be, of free and full pardon and justification; and who are moreover aware that the first step in the Christian life, and prior to its practical and blessed service, is the acceptance of that pardon and justification, that there is but one righteousness that can justify, that such righteousness is the free gift of God, and that submission to that righteousness is the appointed, and only, way of justification in God's sight, should intentionally and systematically abstain from imparting this knowledge to their youthful charge.

The practical advantages and beneficial provisions for time and for eternity of the life of faith are to be sought to be applied to the young human being through precisely the same instrumentality and medium as is appointed for stalwart manhood and hoar old age, the preaching of the gospel.

CHAPTER X.

OBJECT AND MOTIVE.

THE only method of upbringing worthy of the name of Christian, or which is truly consistent with the profession of our most holy faith, must be begun and carried on by instruction in the gospel. It can be in no other way.

To the influence resultant from its acceptance, and operation, as an accepted power, must be submitted, and left entrusted, all those outcomes of behaviour which have to do with the things of time, and which, according to their character, make or mar the earthly career.

The grand paramount and crowning result of its acceptance and belief, that is, of a life consistent with the practical recognition of its truth, is the salvation of the soul; and it is in such a life that provision is to be sought and expected, and there alone found, for befitment for and proper discharge of all the various duties of the present state of existence.

The great end of its teaching is the salvation of the soul, and so it manifestly ought to be taught to the young, as of absolute necessity, and utterly regardless, and altogether independent of any regard to bearings or effects, possible or probable, on the details and interests of this present life.

And this might very well and properly be so, were salvation altogether a thing of the future, and totally absent from and unconnected with the present. But such it is not.

It is in part a work wrought out, and that in the vast majority of instances through long years of present trial, exertion, toil, and suffering, in this earthly sphere.

It is just in this working out of salvation that the believer has to do with the things of time. There a field is furnished for his training for the heavenly inheritance, and it is through the exercise of those very virtues which have been implanted in the heart and soul by the Holy Spirit, as necessary preparatives for a higher state of existence, and as means to the attainment of that holiness 'without which no man shall see the Lord,' that we are to provide for, and anticipate, the faithful discharge of any and all of the duties which may fall to be performed in this present life.

For others, fear, or expediency, or love of gain, or any one or other of the many forms in which unsanctified selfishness may find display, may serve as reason for the honest, decorous, and honourable, before men; but for the believer that discharge of the duties, and employment of the opportunities and advantages of life, which cannot fail to be both pleasing to God and approved of men, is to be sought as the entailed consequence of being influenced by far other and higher aims.

In the course of the development of that salvation which begins with acceptance of pardon and submission to the righteousness of God, and pursues its course 'oft in sorrow, oft in woe,' along the rugged, yet withal happy way of sanctification of body, soul, and spirit, and as, in fact, part of its very operation and application, there are results inevitably consequent on its acceptance with regard to the present period and state of existence.

The fundamental, and all else affecting, of these are the investiture of the life of time with a new object and the inspiration of a new and adequate motive to seek its attainment.

That object is the glory of God, and that motive is love to God.

Nor are these only supplied, but together with them come, in greater or lesser degree, and in more or less rapid course, the ability requisite to yield willing though imperfect obedience to that motive, together with direction and regulation in the display of its effects.

Now it is of the utmost moment to bear in mind that the motive is present before the object is ascertained. In other words, love to God precedes in the mind the loving recognition, and willing adoption, of His glory as the grand object of life.

Furthermore, it is never to be forgotten that our love to God is called into existence, prior of course to its possibly taking the place of a motive, through our being enabled to appreciate, through the enlightening influence of the Holy Spirit, God's love to us.

'We love Him because He first loved us.'

Our love is subsequent to and dependent on our knowledge of God's love to us. It comes as a consequence of such knowledge. We are not born with love to God, it is not indigenous in the human breast, it has to be introduced, and the means by which it is to be introduced are the knowledge and belief of that love which is manifested in the gospel. This is why it is that the preaching of the gospel is the first subject of instruction which should be attended to.

Regarding it solely as a means of inspiring with the sole true motive, it stands to reason that, apart altogether from the manifest necessity of making provision for the eternal interests of the child, the sooner it can be efficaciously applied the better for the individual, even in regard to this present life.

In the moral law of the Mosaic dispensation we are furnished with a compendious directory of human conduct, which is most briefly summed up in the two great generic commandments, 'Thou shalt love the Lord thy God with all thy heart, and with all thy soul, and with all thy strength, and with all thy mind,' and, 'Thou shalt love thy neighbour as thyself.'

That moral law being the declaration of the mind of God as to the regulation of man's conduct during his earthly sojourn, it consequently follows that the keeping of that law, if such a thing were possible, would necessarily induce and maintain the happy equilibrium of moral right and physical health, as well as mental vigour and joy of heart, which the complete discharge of every duty and obligation in the various relationships of life, in accordance with the will of God, must needs involve and secure. Nor is it of any account that it may be suggested that there are details of love enjoined in the Epistles unspecified by name in the more ancient scriptures, for, under the all-inclusive category of 'whatsoever ye would that men should do to you, do ye even so to them,' provision is of necessity made for the most fastidious regard to the most minute details of the most exacting requirements of the most refined, and cultivated, and complex civilization.

The most sanguine of optimists could, having regard to the just and true no less than to the merciful and sentimental, in the idealistic creation of his most brilliant and transcendental of dreams, picture and desire for mankind no more perfect paradise than would be realized in a world-wide keeping of the unchanged, and unchanging, moral law of God.

That and that alone could really satisfy to the

full the honest desires and just aspirations of the truest and highest philanthropy.

Now although it may be possible to apparently approach somewhat near to the keeping of the law by a general outward obedience to its precepts, such attention to the letter of its enactments, though doubtless far from profitless so far as it goes, and however it may be attained and pursued, is something very different to that regard to all the fulness of its exceeding broad requirements, which would seek to obey the very spirit of its enactments, and acknowledge its sovereignty in the realms of inmost thought and secret desire, and which is indispensable to a complete and perfect obedience. Such an obedience it is of course needless to say cannot by any possibility be rendered by any son of Adam, but it is possible to possess a permanent ardent desire of approaching as near to its fulfilment as may be consistent with the weakness and frailty of human nature, weak and frail even under the influence of a true and living faith. And when such a desire is the outcome of love, then it is easy to understand that aiming so high, and under the impelling force of that almost omnipotent of powers, all due allowance being made for the inability inseparably attaching to even the regenerate in their present state of existence, the so-called sinless infirmities of human nature, such a standard of morals may be attained as to render manifest that the non-justifying righteousness of the believer vastly transcends the most zealous, laborious, and painstaking efforts, after the just and the upright, on the part of those who would seek to merit if not to purchase heaven by efforts of their own.

The possession of such a frame of mind is truly and literally supernatural, and utterly beyond the attainment of fallen humanity, save by the miracle-working intervention, and regenerating power, and superhuman influence, and restraining, strengthening, and abiding presence of the Holy Spirit.

Yet such a state of mind is part of the promised heritage of the believer: 'To as many as received Him, to them gave He power to become the sons of God,' 'I will write my laws in their hearts,' and it becomes, more or less rapidly, gradually manifested in the course of the lifelong operation of sanctification.

It is in short to the manifestation of that conduct which is at once a mean to, and the effect of growth in, sanctification that we must look for that training which is to fit the child for the useful and truly successful life.

And we must so look because in the persistent divinely-inspired and sustained endeavour after, and labour in, fulfilling the will of His heavenly Father, and in the consecration of every capacity, power, and energy, to His service, that attitude towards every fellow-creature, that employment and use of every opportunity, will be involved which is the highest realizable ideal of duty.

In the initiation and futhering of the process of sanctification is to be sought that fulfilment of present, and that training for the discharge of future duties, obligations, and relationships, which really constitutes all that is essential in upbringing.

Of course the mere acquisition or imparting of technical knowledge, whether of profession, or art, or handicraft, or the increased proficiency in practical skill attained by the daily training and exercise in its application, however important as matter of detail, must, after all, in the very nature of things, play but a very subsidiary part, as it occupies but a

K

secondary position in order of time, in the great work of upbringing, directed as that is, or at least rightly understood and duly appreciated should be, to that general moral befitment of the subject of its care for a life of usefulness in any of the varied spheres of labour in which man earns his daily bread, or devotes his time and energies to the service of his **God**, on behalf of his fellow-creatures.

As then in the process of sanctification, personal sanctification, as has just been said, is to be sought all that is essential in upbringing, it follows that such a course of instruction as directs and conduces to sanctification must be followed. Now there is but one course recognized in Scripture in which the commencement and working out of sanctification is to be sought, namely as the sequel of justification.

The only way in which justification is possible is through the acceptance of, and submission to, the righteousness of God. There is no other way. So that it accordingly follows that if it is sought to have the work of sanctification, on which must depend that universal and general befitment for life which really constitutes true upbringing, begun and carried on, the child must be taught of the righteousness of God.

In other words, the doctrine of justification by faith is the very first great truth to be made known to the child as the basis of a true gospel upbringing.

CHAPTER XI.

GOSPEL INSTRUCTION.

THE concluding sentence of the immediately preceding chapter may appear to some, perhaps to many, the assertion of a principle the application of which, however desirable if attainable, must be regarded as practically useless, in consequence of the almost insuperable difficulty, if not apparently absolute impossibility, of its reduction to practice.

To demand as the indispensable preliminary to the whole system of upbringing, the inculcation of doctrine, may seem to such preposterous in the extreme.

But if, after all, doctrine is but another name for the statement of truth, when the knowledge of the truth which it expresses is absolutely essential, it manifestly follows that, whether by the higher sounding title of dogma or the simpler appellation of truth, knowledge, the possession of which is indispensable to the attaining of any given end, must be disclosed, if success is to be rendered not only probable but even possible.

Before however proceeding further, it may be as well, in order to avoid any possible misapprehension, to say that in the observations contained in this chapter, as well as in any other portion of this volume, it is not for one moment wished to suggest that any amount of diligence, or display of judgment, in the employment of means, can be of the slightest effect toward the attainment of the desired end, should its successful application be contrary to the inscrutable purposes of God's providence.

It is not to be denied that the most prayerful, zealous, and well-advised instruction in the truth as it is in Jesus may be for years, if not for ever, apparently at least, in vain, and that the best-intentioned, and even best-directed, of efforts to inform the young mind of the love of the Saviour may appear, perhaps to the very hour of death, utterly fruitless labours in a soil seemingly altogether impervious to the softening influences of the gospel message.

With the predeterminate and unknown hidden

purposes of the Almighty it is not for the creature to deal.

But it is for every one who has heard the glad message of mercy, and especially for those who have themselves been led to taste that the Lord is gracious, to obey the injunction that bids them invite others to the gospel feast.

Those who themselves know and believe that they owe all, absolutely all, to sovereign and electing grace, and feel that they themselves have been as it were dragged, or driven, to the foot of the cross, will but wonder, and glorify, and obey. For such the very magnitude of the miracle in their own salvations may even well seem dwarfed by the amazing depth of the love that prompted it.

For such, at all events, it ill becomes to waste or misuse the precious moments of life's short span, seeing in the undeniable though mysterious operation of the eternal purposes of the Most High, if not a reason, at least an excuse for inaction, or a palliative for sloth.

They may not be able to reconcile commandments with mysteries, but they can obey the commandments, and employing the solemn truth of election as a support, and strength, and encouragement, in the hour of their own dire need and extremity, push on, with every effort by the spreading of that knowledge which has been to themselves the passport to safety and joy, to increase the number of those who, as believers, shall in their turns be entitled to similar comfort through the same most reassuring medium. It is for them to scatter abroad the good seed; the result of their labour is with the Ruler of all.

All preaching, from that of the living epistle of the devoted, consistent, and holy life to the declaration of truth by him whose distinctive sphere is that of the especially consecrated and deputed herald of salvation, is subject to one great condition of efficiency, namely that it presents the truth as it really is.

Now in the teaching of the child, which is, all things considered, that department of preaching which if crowned with success is calculated, in all human probability, to be most prolific in happiness and true prosperity, for the simple reason that from the priority of its effect it so early involves all the advantages for time and for eternity of the life of faith, and intercepts so much, although it cannot obviate all, of evil in this present existence, this rule is, it would seem, most happily appropriate, and of manifestly most advantageous application.

The one great panacea for all human ills and woes is the gospel.

But it must be *the* gospel, pure, true, and entire; and a mutilated, or distorted, or false gospel, however near it may seem to approach the true, is not sufficient.

Of the various component parts of the gospel it is unnecessary here to speak. They are assumed to be familiar to the reader. But attention must be directed to the fact that, arranged as they are in the gospel system as enunciated by the voice of inspiration, to transpose the position of the great operations which compose the gospel salvation is not to mar but virtually to nullify the whole.

The two great component parts of the gospel are justification and sanctification, *not* sanctification and justification.

Now *this order* must be observed, or the system enunciated and sought to be followed, though it may be a religious, is not the gospel system. It seems strange that any who themselves entertain correct views of the plan of salvation should tolerate in the teachings of others, much less practise in their own, such a transposition, but that such is in fact very frequently made is sad but true.

It is to this transposition of sanctification into the place of justification that so much that is crude and unsuccessful in the religious, and through the religious in the secular, training of the young may be fairly attributable. Error in the one involves of necessity error in the other, so far indeed as they can be at all treated as separate, for it is difficult to understand how for the believer, whose whole existence is to be one act of prolonged worship and absolutely religious service, any such distinction, as that seemingly implied in the use of the terms religious and secular, really ought to be spoken of as existing, or even treated for one moment as capable of being ascertained or defined.

This error in practice (transposition) may be traceable to one or other of the following causes.

It may be attributable to misunderstanding of the gospel system of salvation, or to the existence of doubts as to its comprehensibility by those of tender years.

Either would in itself amply account for such error. Most probably they generally go together.

Most likely the latter in the vast majority of instances is traceable to the former.

Unbelief in the comprehensibility of the gospel by those of tender years is most probably in a large majority of instances actually caused by misunderstanding of the gospel.

To judge correctly of the feasibility of teaching anything demands not only a just appreciation of the powers of the individual whom it is proposed to instruct, but also a correct acquaintance with the nature of the subject to be taught, and the particulars of that knowledge which it is desired to impart.

It is quite manifest that whether the amount of understanding which can be called into play may be fairly anticipated as sufficient to comprehend any given subject must be determined by a consideration of the nature of that subject, and the ability to master must be gauged by a correct estimate of the difficulties to be overcome.

So then, unless the subject be known and understood, it is not to be expected that a correct judgment can be arrived at as to the ability of a pupil for its reception.

No one who did not know the gospel message

could possibly determine whether it could be understood by a child.

The teaching children the moral law and the drilling them up in a strict observance of a seemly ritual of praise and worship, perhaps the urging, it may even be with ill-befitting austerity of demeanour, the paramount duty of love to God, these and such-like species of religious instruction they neither disdain nor neglect, but the gospel itself, the glad tidings of a heavenly Father perfectly reconciled in a loving Saviour, and *absolutely irreconcilable in any other way*, and the news of that *gift* of never-ending life which has been presented to man in Christ Jesus our Lord, are looked upon as things above and beyond their understandings, topics on which it is premature and useless, if not even unwise, to discourse.

Far transcending as it may the profoundest contemplation of the most exalted of created intelligences, in what may for lack of fitter expression be termed the philosophy of its occurrence, the gospel, as regards some perception of its practical benefits and the manner of their appropriation by the individual sinner, is not beyond the understanding of the child of ordinary intelligence, listening with rapt attention at a mother's knee to the story of a Saviour's love.

Of course there is a limit of years up to which it is impossible to explain the rudiments of the gospel, just as there is an age up to which it is impossible to teach anything.

In that extreme period of earliest childhood it must needs suffice to entrust the tender heart to the covenanted mercies of the God and Redeemer of its parents, but the period of sufficient comprehension dawns much earlier upon the youthful mind than the conduct of many would lead us to suppose, and it is the duty of the parent or instructor, far from deferring to a more convenient season the pointing of that confiding eye to the cross of Calvary, to watch eagerly, and with prayerful solicitude, for the earliest available opportunity to engrave God's glorious character, as the Pardoner and Justifier, upon the comparatively tender and unpreoccupied heart of childhood.

Such an opportunity may be expected, in the natural order of events, in the child of average intelligence at a very early period. Recognition of the existence of individuals, itself the result of observation, is followed by the personal identification of such individuals. That enables to comprehend and appreciate the existence of any person once seen though for the time absent.

The exercise of this latter ability is of course early, very early, familiar to the child.

So soon as able to understand and realize the existence of any unseen individual, so as to be able to converse reasonably respecting them, the mind is, if not actually in, at least not very far from a condition of development to hear with profit of Him who is

'Now ascended up on high.'

His existence as a real living human Being once made part of the child's stock of knowledge, and the Saviour thus introduced amidst those other persons with whose existence the child is familiar, it next comes with the utmost convenient and practicable speed to teach the same lesson as that which was addressed to the Philippian jailer, that of present, absolute trust in this living Person, this great unseen Friend.

Absolute trust in a person naturally prepares for, and leads up to, the announcement of his will as the necessary preliminary to acting in accordance with his behests, and so availing oneself of his friendly and proffered aid.

Jesus known to the child as the great unseen Friend who alone can save, it follows most naturally to tell the child what is to be done in order to follow the directions of this Saviour, in other words, to preach the gospel in respect of how it is to be obeyed and so to show *how* He saves.

Now it is here that the moral law comes to our aid. Not however as a directory for detailed obedience whereby either to strive to please God or win eternal life.

The knowledge of the moral law is to be employed in its application to a child, just as to the as yet unbelieving adult, to convince of sin, to manifest the utter futility of any attempt to win salvation by keeping it, and to demonstrate the absolute necessity of salvation through the work of Another.

The gospel is in its very essence salvation by substitution.

Whether so understood and duly recognized or not, whether so explained or not, there it really and unalterably remains, and in the very nature of things must ever remain, a system of salvation through substitution.

The inception of its force upon the human heart, alike of child as of adult, as a beneficent and sanctifying power, is the immediate, perhaps so immediate as to appear simultaneous, consequence of the recognition of there having been effected, through the substitution of the sacrifice and satisfaction and righteousness of another, an absolute present and complete reconciliation with our heavenly Father.

Perfect acceptance in God's sight on the basis of the finished work of another is the first step in the Christian life.

The gospel accepted and believed is invincible, because its strength is derived not from human qualification or exertion, but from the pledged power of the Almighty.

But just as a course of curative treatment demands not only the most scrupulous attention to the composition of the medicines to be employed, but also the strictest adherence to the prescribed order of their administration, and the way for the crowning remedy is opened up by a carefully arranged, and absolutely indispensable, course of preparation, it is necessary in the application of the great gospel remedy to adhere with like undeviating care, and scrupulous precision, to the advice and direction of the great Divine Physician.

If the unspeakable benefits, temporal as well as eternal, accruing from the enjoyment of the effects characteristic of and dependent on the progress of personal sanctification are desired, they are to be attained only through the prior acceptance of the *gift* of justification.

Such is the scriptural order of precedence, and such, and no other, can consequently be the true.

Now, how is justification attainable? Simply and solely through accepting of Christ as our Substitute.

The only justification is that attained through faith. Nor does the comparative immunity from actual sin in the case of a child, as we very well know, go to invalidate in the least its full necessity for that sole, complete, and absolutely free justification.

No matter with whatsoever plausibility the suggestions of pride and unbelief may point to the comparative guilelessness, and simplicity, and winning lovableness, and endearing confidence of the child. Though all these may exist, together with them there co-exists as absolute a necessity in degree for the all-sufficient justifying work of Jesus, as in the case of the sin-begrimed and wrinkled convict, for whom the morrow will bring the scaffold and the grave of shame.

It may not indeed be agreeable to proud humanity in the hearts of the world without, but, just as any other advance of that false and meretricious liberality of indifference, which nowadays would seem so often to usurp the place of honour, even in the temple of the Most High, in the heart of the believer it may not be suffered to linger, much less be permitted to abide.

The believer's estimate, despite the fair and insinuating sophistries of lying sentimentality, must be the scriptural estimate; and is, that the guileless mien of childhood in reality covers, though it may be perchance full ofttimes well conceals, the heart and soul of a born, hateful, and already condemned rebel.

For the babe as for the adult Jesus has lived and died. Had He not, that babe must have breathed but to have been lost.

L

But to return from these digressions.

It has been already pointed out that the child, having been made acquainted with and enabled to realize the existence of the Saviour as an actually living though unseen Person, and taught to look to Him as such, is now naturally in the position to hear His words, and to learn *in what respects and how He has become and is* a Saviour. This resolves itself into an explanation of the practical application of the doctrine of justification by faith. Such explanation is to be made by the declaration and specific explanation of the nature and effects of our blessed Lord and Saviour's substitutionary work.

Now this is not of course meant to imply that any attempt to explain what may be termed the philosophy, or even the theory, of substitution is called for.

The former is impossible and the latter is unnecessary.

It is *the knowledge of its practical application* that is to be imparted to and sought to be impressed on the youthful mind.

This of course invites, nay further involves, the narration of the history of those lifelong and death-consummated labours and sufferings through which only it became possible.

It is manifest that before the need of substitutionary satisfaction for sin can be made intelligible, not to say appreciated as indispensable to personal safety, it must be shown that there is such a thing as sin. It must be moreover shown in what it consists, or rather what constitutes it, and its presence, influence, effects, and inevitable consequences, if unatoned for, must be made plain and unmistakeable.

Now the Holy Spirit alone can convince of personal sin and wield the almighty power that shows salvation to be the one great necessity of existence, as well as with mighty, sudden, irresistible impulse, or more gradually soul-pervading influence of overpowering suasion compel to its acceptance.

He alone can pour upon naturally purblind humanity the light of spiritual perception, and bend the will and inspire the power to lay hold upon eternal life freely offered to us in the gospel.

But in this as in the various other manifestations of His power and goodness, the Almighty deigns to employ appointed means.

Now the knowledge of the law is the means to prepare for the reception of the gospel, in that through it is shown the absolute necessity of just precisely such a remedy as is therein and *therein only* to be found.

It describes in specific terms the requirements and nature of that obedience which is demanded from man by his Maker as the condition of life.

In so doing it shows what that righteousness must be which is necessary to constitute a man just in the sight of God.

When treated as a system of requirement so incapable of disintegration, in its indissolubly compacted unification, that the breach or neglect of any single particular of its component demands is a breach or neglect of the whole, and when moreover received in the exceeding breadth of that comprehensiveness which embraces not only the overt act but the faintest movement of desire, demanding absolute and perfect obedience in thought, word, and deed, it should seem hardly conceivable but that the *veriest child*, if but made truly acquainted with its demands, could fail to acknowledge his sin and confess his guilt.

The great first office of the law in relation to the gospel economy is to convince of sin.

There is another and subsequent employment of the law, as a detailed exposition of the will of our heavenly Father, of use to guide the believer as a practical rule in life, but of such employment as a means to personal sanctification it is not now necessary to treat.

The command is not to teach the law but to preach the gospel, and the law is only to be mentioned in the preaching of the gospel prior to its avowed acceptance by the individual addressed, as a mean to elucidate the necessity for the gospel, and render its acceptance manifestly indispensable to salvation.

This purpose of the law achieved, sin declared, and defined, and brought home, the eye is to be directed at once to the cross of Christ, and the blessed and life-inspiring news proclaimed that thereon the work of satisfying and keeping this same law to the minutest detail was once and for ever finished for every believer.

Nor that alone. The further truth is to be announced that it is only by accepting this as true and believing it, that is by living consistently with its being true and actually and unavoidably directly affecting himself and his own individual case, that *any* son of Adam can please God.

It is to be clearly and absolutely taught that God has declared that it is only by any one accepting of this keeping of the law by Jesus instead of trying to keep it for himself that he can be looked upon by God as having kept it, and continuing to keep it.

It is to be clearly and absolutely taught that now instead of endeavouring to keep the law for ourselves, in order to be regarded by God as righteous, *we are to accept of this righteousness* which has been **wrought out for us by our Saviour.**

It is to be clearly and absolutely taught that now not only is any attempt to keep the law for ourselves in order to be regarded by God as just not only an absolute waste of time but an act of positive sin.

It is to be shown that such conduct is a refusal to benefit by the lifelong and dying sufferings of God's own Son. It is to be pointed out that so to act is to reject the only possible means of accepting the gift of eternal life. It is to be represented as a sinning against our own mercies. It is to be treated as making God a liar. Finally, it is to be taught, and sought by every available means to be instilled, that *the* great sin to be dreaded is that special form of unbelief which will not accept the gospel offer of full and free salvation to the uttermost for the sake of Jesus' finished work.

It may be said that such teaching is very well for the grown up, but quite beyond the child. It may be said that it is quite impossible for a child to comprehend such a system of substitution.

Well, after all, the child is not asked to comprehend it. The child is to be taught to accept, submit to, and believe, that is, just *obey* it. It is undeniably perfectly possible to believe what you cannot comprehend.

Belief is simply action or conduct consistent with, and in dependence on, an accepted state of facts and circumstances.

The test of capacity sufficient to receive such teaching is not the capability of comprehending the theory of substitution, but the ability to accept of its practical aid and working.

If a child is fit to be taught *any* commandment with the reasonable hope that he can understand it so far as to endeavour to keep it, how is he unable to understand that some one else has received a precisely similar command?

If he can understand the keeping or attempt to keep a commandment on the part of himself, why can he not realize the keeping of or attempt to keep it by another?

If he can understand so much, what is to prevent him realizing, if a little care is taken and a little patience expended, that this other's doing is on his behalf, or instead of his own, and can serve for his advantage and benefit as well as if it had been his own?

If he can understand anything whatever being done, at all, why should he not understand it to be done for his advantage although by another? Why, surely, the very appeal of the child to the felt superior strength and ability of the parent might sufficiently serve to exemplify, if not even to some extent to explain, the substitutionary work of our blessed Saviour.

The very appeal for the blossomed branch, that hangs far beyond the reach of his own little arm, might serve, and that most opportunely, to place within his grasp the fruit of the Living Vine.

So soon as the child is capable of receiving *any*

commandment, instead of his being taught the moral law, let him be taught the commandment of the law of faith.

Let him be taught, and taught *as a command*, to believe on the Lord Jesus Christ; and as the very first step in the development of such belief, let him be taught the paramount duty and absolute necessity of submission to the righteousness of God.

'Christ is the end of the law for righteousness to every one that believeth.' And even when, in the loving and earnest endeavours to secure at the earliest possible moment every available inch of vantage-ground for the future struggle, it is sought to impress upon the mind of the child the words of eternal wisdom, ere yet any reasonable hope may be entertainable of their meaning being comprehended, such opportunity should be seized to impress upon the yet vacant tablets of memory the verbal outline of the gospel of grace, as the best conceivable available preliminary to that better inculcation and explanation, the fitting time for which, whilst prayerfully and anxiously longed for, is at the same time to be trustfully and patiently awaited.

But there may after all exist in the minds of many who neither doubt the necessity of precisely the same justification for their children as for themselves, or even mistrust the capacity of the youthful mind to adequately grasp the practical application of free pardon and the righteousness of God, as the sole means by which it is to be enjoyed, another, and in their opinion, most potent reason for withholding the true and free gospel from their children.

It is not that they entertain any fallacious views as to the necessity of any preparation for the reception of the gospel save the sense of its felt need.

But they do entertain feelings of grave mistrust as to the propriety, or rather indeed safety, of entrusting what they cannot help regarding as a knowledge of divine grace, *free* grace, to the mind as yet premature for such a discovery of freedom.

They fear to entrust the child with the knowledge that salvation is all of grace lest such knowledge should be misused.

They are afraid, in short, lest they should thereby deliberately expose their children to the risk of turning the grace of God into lasciviousness. It may well be that after all *this* is, with many, the actual reason for refraining from truly gospel instruction of the young.

They fear inculcating something which they dread under the name Antinomianism. The very dread of dishonouring the law positively leads to their actually doing so!

For the believer they know that the law, as a means of justification in the sight of God by personal exertion, does not exist; would that they equally recognized that it is in the sanctified walk of the believer that it is indeed most nearly fulfilled!

Devoutest reverence is not synonymous with, or displayed in, the fearfulness of unbelief. To reject or refrain from that course of procedure which has not only been sanctioned but positively enjoined as absolutely and indispensably necessary, is to tempt the Most High.

To deliberately withhold, on *any* ground, those tidings which they have been commanded to proclaim, is manifest *disobedience*.

Nor does it alter the character of such conduct that it is sought, or may even appear, to be defended on grounds of probable utility.

It is for the believer to obey, and, in obeying, employ that very mean which the omniscience and love of our heavenly Father has appointed, and in the use of which the creature is alone entitled to expect the rich, though it may be ofttimes long-deferred, downpour of promised blessing.

Prudence in spiritual matters must be *spiritual* prudence.

Conversion is not the work of man. The seemingly most perfectly suitable of human agencies, however admirable in its apparent adaptation to do God's work, can of itself effect nothing.

Conversion is a miracle, and in order to work that miracle the gospel remedy must be applied. Not *a* gospel but *the* gospel must be preached. Free grace is not to be kept back from the child, any more than from the man, because, forsooth, in human judgment, it may be thought dangerous. Even in respect to the affairs of time, timidity is ofttimes ruin, in respect to those of eternity it may lead to absolute destruction. It is saddening to think with what fearfully solemn consequences the supposed prudence of pious humility may have ofttimes in reality been the, albeit unrecognized, arrogance of unbelieving and audacious presumption.

Would that, over the broad area of professing Christendom, were fully realized by every parent and preceptor the fearful danger that is oft incurred, no less really because so often it may be all unconsciously, through faithless diffidence or fallacious mistrust, of practically neglecting, if not absolutely despising, the gracious counsel and loving invitation given long years ago in distant Galilee:

'Suffer little children to come unto me, and forbid them not.'

It is possible, too possible, whilst seeming, and even desiring, to obey, virtually to disregard, if not positively to impede, the fulfilment of this injunction by neglecting, or forbearing, to announce as removed those barriers to trustful, loving, and present access, which have been long since for ever completely swept away, through the bitter travails and glorious consummation of our Saviour's finished work.

CHAPTER XII.

JUSTIFICATION AND SANCTIFICATION.

THE results to be anticipated from the pursuance of a system of gospel instruction such as has been sketched out in the preceding pages are just such as may be fairly looked for whenever, in any undertaking, success has been duly courted by reasonable attention, in its carrying out, to the guiding principles of judgment and truth.

Success may be fairly expected, so far as its enjoyment may be in accordance with the Divine will, in this instance because by such a system of procedure recourse is had to the only power equal to the achievement of the end desired.

Moreover, what is for practical purposes equally important, such power is thereby employed and applied in the appointed way, and with due attention to the fulfilment of those conditions without the strict observance of which it is virtually *not* employed, although to the ignorant, casual, or superficial observer it may seem to be.

Without due regard to the relative positions allotted to justification and sanctification in the gospel system, such neglect is manifested, not only of the demands of the innate necessity of fallen and lost human nature, and of the varied exigencies of the present life, but also of the absolute requirements and peremptory injunctions of gospel teaching, as cannot fail to constitute such deviation from, although unaccompanied by avowed rejection of, the course dictated and alone authorized by sound doctrine as must needs, in the ordinary current of events, lead to disappointment, disaster, and loss.

Plausible and pleasing as may appear any scheme of quasi-gospel relief and reformation, if thereby the attempt, needless as vain, and illogical as impossible of success, is made to attain to sanctification save as subsequent to, and resultant from, justification, however or how long soever such efforts may appear successful in ameliorating the spiritual condition, and in even actually amending the external moral life, and whatever pleas of utility or expediency may be urged for its acceptance, it is to deprecated, rejected, and opposed as absolutely repugnant to sound doctrine.

Such is any plan which would aim at the attainment of sanctification prior to the acceptance of justification.

It does not affect the matter, in the least, to point to the undeniable fact that it does not unfrequently happen that amendment of life, and attention to religious duties and observances, the grievous and painful exertions and strivings of ignorance and self-righteousness, frequently too perhaps the result and development of erroneous teaching, do often precede the breaking of the true day.

It is nothing to the point to call attention to the fact that the first gropings of the startled soul are ofttimes, it may be said instinctively, after a holy life as a means of justification, or rather at any rate perhaps as a preparation for justification, or that such endeavours and such solicitude would even at times appear to prepare the way for the message of peace.

With that we have no more to do than with the discussion of any other aspect of the question of the permitted existence of evil.

That He who 'maketh the wrath of man to praise Him' can, and frequently does, lead the soul by devious and apparently most unlikely paths to the strait gate, is but one of those unfathomable mysteries which as far transcend our comprehension as they are manifestly to be excluded from our calculations.

A course of action has been prescribed for our guidance, and to frame our endeavours in manifest and direct opposition to its requirements can never be justly defended as right and proper, because forsooth such procedure has been sometimes, or even frequently, observed to be followed by happy results.

Such results are not attributable to the erroneous teachings, and fallacious treatment, and wayward wanderings which have preceded them, but to the advent of that almighty grace which exposes and refutes error, neutralizes evil, and directs aright.

But that method of procedure which is in accordance with the enlightened discernment of the truth of the gospel, and is arranged for the just and consistent application of its remedy to the youthful heart, and soul, and mind, can be followed, not only in the cheering and inspiring knowledge that God's work is being attempted in God's prescribed way, but also in the enjoyment of the inestimable satisfaction that, whatever the ultimate event, its adopter can surely anticipate, even in the grief of failure, the absence of an untowardly accusing conscience.

The pursuance of a plan which gives to justification and to sanctification each its just, because scripturally appointed, place in gospel upbringing, is in truth the only reasonable method of setting about the great work of befitting the child for the truly successful use and enjoyment of existence.

It is so because it, and it alone, accepts things as they truly are.

It starts from the adoption as its basis of the true position of absolute dependence on the Creator which humanity occupies.

It acknowledges the true relationship existing between the things of time and the concerns of eternity.

It duly appreciates these in so far that the former are subordinate to the latter, as of invincible necessity.

It recognizes the continuity of existence in that true appreciation of the present life, with all its pretensions, which regards it as but the portal to a never-ending future.

It accepts the scriptural estimate of unregenerate, unsanctified, human nature as absolutely and literally true.

It regards heart, soul, and mind as defiled and fallen, and in themselves utterly impotent, even if willing, to satisfy the demands of Divine justice even when supported and vouched by the most awe-inspiring sense of impending judgments, and much less capable of rendering the acceptable homage of a perfect, willing, devoted, and unrestrained obedience.

It acknowledges at the same time that only in such a course of lifelong loving service can be found that submission to the sway of the universal government of the Most High which can induce and enable to that employment of the opportunities, and enjoyment of the benefits, of time which alone can ensure the truly joyous, albeit perhaps not always visibly or presently or tangibly successful, earthly career.

Then above all it accepts (as, in acknowledgment and belief of these truths, as well as of the all-sufficient and tender love of God in Christ, it cannot but accept) the sole possible all-providing remedy as to be found only in that proffered **free** grace which pardons, cleanses, justifies, and consecrates, and, having consecrated, induces to and empowers for that loving, willing, and hearty submission to the behests of the law of faith, through, and in, which the Almighty Spirit works out the crowning triumph of present grace, and indispensable befitment for future glory, in the advancing development of personal sanctification.

The effect of the acceptance and belief (be it ever borne in mind, but another word for the consistent application of acknowledged truth) of these principles in the conduct of the upbringing of the young, or at least the object aimed at, (for of course it were presumption to assert that the best directed of efforts must of necessity be crowned either immediately or even ever with success), is to bring the child at the earliest possible moment into that state of reconciliation with our heavenly Father, through submission to His revealed will in the acceptance of free, full, and absolute justification for the sake of Christ's finished work, which is the necessary and sole prelude to that course of personal sanctification, wherein the temporal and incidental benefits of the life of faith are to be attained.

The temporal advantages accruing to the believer in the course of his life of loving obedience must ever be regarded as, in measure at least, purely incidental, for though it is true that 'godliness hath the promise of this life,' it is false to hold that 'gain is godliness.' 'The kingdom of heaven is not meat and drink.'

The general directory for such employment of the present life's opportunities and advantages as amounts to 'using as not abusing,' for the term world may most conveniently and surely, without any unjustifiable stretch of meaning, be taken to stand for every detail of that existence the enjoyment of which is involved in the possibility of use or abuse, has been at least since Mosaic times the moral law.

Although of course with that law as a means of justification in the sight of God the believer has absolutely nothing to do, for 'Christ is the end of the law for righteousness to every one that believeth,' it affords as a rule of life the absolutely perfect standard of earthly existence, and supplies the grand summary of Christian ethics.

In the observance of its precepts is to be found that ordering of life to be eagerly desired and followed by every believer as commensurate if not literally synonymous with the discharge of every Christian duty, because in the fulfilment of its varied obligations is found the practical and detailed manifestation of perfect love.

'Whoso loveth his neighbour hath fulfilled the law, for love is the fulfilling of the law.'

The perfect display then of the greatest and most enduring of the Christian graces is to be found, not in some fanciful will-worship or fantastic pseudo-philanthropy, robbing it may be to pay, but in the fulfilling of the law.

Once indeed, and once only, long since absolutely kept and fully honoured by our Blessed Lord and Saviour in the labours and sufferings necessary for our redemption, that law is now to be honoured in the persons of those whom He has redeemed, as their willingly and lovingly accepted rule of life. To none other can it be such.

And yet superior, because fuller, as the manifestation of the sole way of salvation (that salvation itself ever the same) is in the clear sunshine of the Christian era to its far-off though yet sufficient display in the dim light of patriarchal or later ceremonial worship, with its reign of mysterious types and shadows, so too the everlasting law itself, illumined by the rays of the Sun of righteousness, and the application of its spirit as well as of its letter to the multitudinous requirements of life, when the deeper meaning of its provisions has been revealed, explained, and, so to speak, amplified by the enriching gloss and elucidating commentaries of the New Testament, has become, in the teaching of the Holy Spirit, a far more specifically and clearly detailed revelation of the guiding will of Heaven in matters of everyday morality.

That love which had all along been present, the real though perhaps but rarely recognized inspirer of justice, is now publicly revealed in all the serene majesty of power, and installed sovereign arbiter in every question even to the most refined casuistic necessity of busy life.

Once brought to look for justification, complete and absolute, solely to the finished work of Christ, and so entitled to the possession of that power to become the child of God which is indispensable to the willing to perform no less than to the performance of its requirements, the child is now *under the law to Christ.*

Henceforth it is to be brought up 'in the nurture and admonition of the Lord.'

Such nurture and admonition is to be derived of course through Scripture. More especially in the first instance from the New Testament.

'All scripture is given by inspiration of God, and is profitable for reproof, for correction, and for instruction in righteousness;' but the employment of its counsel and power, unless unmistakeably otherwise directed, must surely but be in accordance with the judgment of sound, and spiritually enlightened, reason.

It was through the intervention of apostolic, and apostolically authorized or recognized, teaching that the first knowledge of the rudimentary truths of the gospel was diffused abroad amongst mankind.

Such knowledge of salvation once published and received, the Epistles were addressed to those who had already 'fled for safety to the Hope set before them in the Gospel.'

As has been already pointed out, they were not addressed primarily to the world at large.

Whatever their incidental value and availability as exponents of the religion of the cross, in the domain of what may be described as scientific theology, and however they may be adapted for the instruction of those without as well as the strengthening of those within, or however calculated, in like manner as the moral law, through their exposition of the claims and requirements of justice, purity, and truth, to startle to a sense of danger, and demonstrate the need of a Saviour, they were, in matters whether of faith, doctrine, or practice, primarily addressed to believers, and so they must be still.

Now, 'nurture and admonition,' if conducted in strict accordance with the sentiments, admonitions, and injunctions of the New Testament, and so directed to the fulfilment of the requirements and obligations of the moral law, expounded as it is so to speak in the gospel light by the announcement of the new commandments of the final revelation of love, will be declared and manifested in a system of upbringing very different indeed, not only in aim but also in motive, to that approved and popular in the eyes of worldly wisdom.

Such a system will needs be radically and unavoidably different from such other in the arrangement of its procedure, as well as in the mode of its application, however the external effects of their respective employments may seem to resemble or coincide, or may even actually agree in temporary results, or partake of correlative benefits.

Manifest, perhaps even dazzling, success, and that in the most restricted and literal acceptation and application of the term, may crown alike the earthly careers of two lives, the one conducted in accordance with the spirit and, so far as may be, the letter of the gospel rule, the other one long immolation on the altar of absolute and uncompromising selfishness and mammon-worship.

And just as success, vouchsafed in material or visible prosperity, may be apparent in the case of the believer as well as of the unbeliever, so in the absolutely technical preparation necessary to enable to win the means of subsistence or befit to discharge any of those multifarious duties of life which may fall to the lot of any one, whether treading the broad or the narrow way, the same necessary special training must be common in the case of either.

It is not therefore in manifest distinction as regards the subjects-matter of instruction that the distinct and well-defined line of demarcation between the teaching of the gospel and the training of the world is always to be sought or can always be found.

It is present in the difference of the motives from which these various labours are undertaken, and of the manners in which they are sought to be carried on.

Nor is such difference to be sought, or expected to be very clearly, if at all, exhibited or very precisely defined, in the matter or manner of satisfying those prominent and peremptory demands of situation, where the discharge of duty is generally, if not universally and of necessity, practically coincident with the fulfilling the requirements and yielding to the solicitations of self-interest.

Much in the present life all mankind must necessarily have in common.

The literal fulfilment and outward observance of the second table of the moral law is so absolutely and manifestly essential to the very existence of society, and the enjoyment of personal freedom and comfort, to say nothing of material prosperity, that the very cravings of selfishness and exigencies of carnal policy demand its external observance. And when the long-continued sway of these general demands, strengthened and countenanced moreover by the presence of the gospel in truth and power in the lives of many around, has prepared the way for the safe, convenient, and advantageous display, at will, of those details of obedience to the requirements of the second table of the moral law which, ofttimes at really little cost, go to render life more pleasant and enjoyable, by softening its asperities and conducing, if not positively inviting, to the luxurious enjoyment of the welcome returns of loud-resounding gratitude, much even of the more minutely expressed external morality of the gospel dispensation may be found appropriated into the practical ethics of purely carnal and mundane policy.

But 'how can two walk together unless they be agreed?'

There is a point where innate corruption and the spirit of the world combine to resist, and beyond which they will *not* go.

So long as human pride can, without loss of personal dignity and with advantage to her sister lusts, and compeer vices, appropriate or utilize, to a degree, the suggestions of heavenly wisdom with regard to the conduct of the affairs of time, and so enjoy any inseparable temporal benefits obtainable by so doing, the world and the Church may seem to labour side by side, in zealous harmony, in the interests of our race.

But when not only are objects specified but the methods by which their attainments are to be sought are prescribed to the exclusion of all other, and such methods are so contrary to preconceived notions and opposed to natural instincts, nay more than opposed, so repugnant to unregenerate human nature, as to entail the absolute repudiation of its judgments, and crucifixion of its darling tendencies and cherished desires, it can surely be little wonder that the servants of mammon should throw off even the semblance of allegiance to the King of kings.

This of course should matter but little, nay might even appear, in some respects at least, an event to be desired rather than regretted; for, as a general rule, such alliances are manifestly far more likely to be productive of temporal benefit to the world than of spiritual advantage to the Church.

Even the undeniable superficial improvements in

the customs and circumstances of life accruing to society at large through the assimilations, from wrong motives, of worldly policy to the requirements of gospel morality may, unless subsequently sanctified by the Holy Spirit to the right use of their employers, lead to little anticipated and most untoward results.

But it is quite possible for the children of light to seek the attainment of objects specified, in ways very different to those prescribed, without either assuming the attitude of undisguised insubordination to their Lord and Master, or openly and avowedly deserting His cause.

They may, whilst remaining true at heart and still deeply solicitous for His interests, endeavour to conduct the operations of their warfare against evil (and be it ever borne in mind that upbringing involves much warfare against evil) in accordance with principles, more or less, at variance with the declarations of His revealed will.

They may virtually 'do evil that good may come.'

They certainly would frequently seem to do so in reference to the upbringing of the young.

They would seem therein not uncommonly to

even seek to accomplish righteousness by the means of sin, through the accepted and authorized employment of sin as an agent.

Turning to passages in the New Testament wherein are enumerated various forms of iniquity, it will be found that side by side with those open and gross violations of the law of love which directly affect the interests of truth, the enjoyment of life, the preservation of purity, and the rights of property, there are specified certain states of mind, or developments of desire and passion, which as influencing motives, however accepted, fostered, and utilized (it may even be admired and lauded as desirable and advantageous, if not even indispensable instruments in the successful prosecution of the affairs of time), are there in the most unmistakeable and unqualified manner defined and denounced as sins.

It follows, however unpalatably, as an unavoidable consequence that whenever, or wherever, any one of these is employed as a means, or utilized as an aid, to the accomplishment of any end, no matter how proper in itself, a specific sin is actually, if not avowedly or wittingly, employed as a servant or accepted as an ally.

Love of prosperity is one of those natural instincts for which, as for the gratification of other desires innocent in themselves and not only conducive to the comfort and usefulness of the individual possessor, but also more or less directly contributory to the benefit of the species, ample provision has been made in the economy of life by the all-merciful 'Giver of every good and every perfect gift.'

But just as in the case of any other of the longings and requirements of humanity for which a lawful outlet has been provided and a way appointed whereby alone its gratification may be sought, whilst upon every other the ban of heaven's displeasure has been unmistakeably set, so to seek prosperity by devious paths, or endeavour after its attainment by means which the teachings of the gospel forbid, is not only to incur present guilt but also to involve sooner or later, in the ordinary course of events, the certainty of unavoidable hurt and trouble.

Prosperity may itself be abused, and it is whenever its possession is prostituted by subserviency to any other end than that of the glory of God, including of course, needs it be said, the loving exertions of faith on behalf of the best and truest interests of our fellow-creatures.

After all, moreover, prosperity may not be in every case, or always in like degree, in accordance with the Divine will, and, as is by no means unfrequently the case, the lot of the undoubtedly beloved favourite of heaven may be cast amid toil, disappointment, trouble, anguish, and failure in regard to the things of this life.

Still, accepting prosperity as not only allowably desirable and as a general rule in some degree attainable in the ordinary course of events as a necessary result of the discharge of duty, and when, moreover, desired from a proper motive, that is the honest and pure intention of its consecration to the glory of God, a worthy object of desire, it may still be sought by ways so contrary to the revealed will of God that it shall be found, when obtained, to bear the indelible impress and ineffaceable stain of those sins which have been made instrumental in its attainment.

Assuming that a parent has been in the hands of the Holy Spirit the honoured instrument, by due attention to the truth of the gospel, of enabling the child to look to Jesus alone for salvation, and to accept the propitiation for his sins and the working out of that righteousness by the acceptance of which he can alone be justified as past and completely finished works, and that henceforth the acknowledged and avowed object of life is sanctification, 'the perfecting holiness in the fear of the Lord,' of course, as has been already said, the nurture and admonition which is to conduce to this end is to be primarily sought in the teachings of the New Testament.

Now as the work of upbringing is thus made absolutely identical with instruction for, together with guidance and aid in, sanctification, every rule of life applicable to the effecting of sanctification becomes immediately, so far as may be applicable, binding in the case of the child.

If there were indeed any sins specially restricted in the possibility of their commission to years of maturity or manhood or old age, with regard to such there might be some show of reason in deferring the dealing till a future and more appropriate season.

But if such a course could almost seem excusable, or might even possibly appear not only judicious, but at times and in cases justifiable, with reference to the sins of overt impurity, or fraud, or avarice, no such conduct could at any time or under any circumstances be admissible with regard to sins against justice, mercy, or truth.

Nor is such disregard any more allowable as to the sins of provocation, envy, hatred, malice, emulation, and the pursuit of vainglory, placed as these latter are in the infallible judgment of inspiration in close proximity with what the universal verdict of mankind readily recognizes as the indisputably heinous and flagitious enormities of murder, rapine, and lust.

That covetousness, envy, and the pursuit of vainglory, however readily condoned or made light of in the judgment of the world, or even as is too frequently the case actually invoked and fostered, in some one or other of the various shapes, frequently it may be disguises, which they are capable of assuming, as powerful and valuable energy-inspiring factors in the competitions of school, and subsequent, life, are really as actually and truly sins as murder, adultery, and fornication, it is but necessary to recall to mind the counsels of our Blessed Lord and Saviour, or to refer to such categories of wickedness or specific injunctions as are to be met with in the Epistles to the Romans (i. 29), Galatians (v. 19, 20, 21, and 26), Ephesians (iv. 31, and v. 3), Philippians (ii. 3), Colossians (iii. 5), Titus (iii. 3), Hebrews (xiii. 5), James (iii. 14, and iv. 1), 1 Peter (ii. 1, and 11), 2 Peter (i. 4), or elsewhere.

As sins then, and sins which are capable of commission in the early years of childhood, to declare as soon as possible their wickedness, and seek to restrain and conquer their power, is manifestly the duty of every parent and preceptor of youth.

Even were they not essentially sins, but with truth capable of being regarded as mere regretable infirmities, or easily pardonable weaknesses of human nature, having regard to the unrest, discomfort, and misery, which their presence, to any extent, entails, to the fearful certainty of the growth of their influence, if neglected, and the possible results of their continued indulgence, culminating it may be some day in the perpetration of some enormity of guilt, wherein sin shall manifest its dire and appalling heinousness in the eyes of mankind in the commission of open and recognized crime, common sense might be thought equal to suggest the peremptory advisability of barring, so far as may be their entrance, or, if they are already to be found within, striving to the utmost to neutralize their influence and crush their power.

It is not thus, however, that they are generally treated.

They are, as matter of fact, not only very generally tolerated, but actually sought to be utilized, and that by not a few who profess to conduct the upbringing of the young in strictest accordance with the principles of the Christian religion.

It would seem that in the minds of such there exists, whether as a result of imperfect personal realization of the truth, or from deference to long-established custom, or from the influence of scholastic tradition, or from fear of offending long-established, though ill-founded prejudices, a conviction that these real sins are, up to a certain degree, or when turned judiciously to account, and that for ends in themselves permissible or desirable, capable of being indulged without danger, and if employed for the purpose of rousing or stimulating the ambition, or latent energy of the child, are even transmuted from vices into virtues.

So it comes to pass that those very passions, which when displayed in the full and devastating development of some instance of a matured ambition gratifying, through havoc, bloodshed, and ruin, its unrestrained pride of heart and lust of power appal and horrify, are, from failure to detect them in the subtle natures of their beginnings, solicitously cherished in embryo to gladden the fond home circle by the winning of a trumpery school prize.

For the gratification of parental pride with its darling visions of fame and distinction, or to satisfy a teacher's greed of gain or desire of importance and credit, the school life of the child is, often from a very early period, arranged and conducted to a large extent in accordance with principles plainly at variance with the letter, and utterly opposed to the spirit of gospel teaching.

If there is one object of endeavour more strongly denounced in the Bible than almost any other, it is the indulgence and gratification of pride, and almost if not equally so, is the desire of vainglory.

Yet it requires but the slightest exertion of analytical acumen, if indeed any investigation, however slight, of motives or designs, is necessary when the truth, if not candidly avowed, is so very readily patent to even the most casual and superficial of observers, to be convinced beyond reasonable doubt, that the gratification of pride, or the thirst after vainglory, occupies after all, in the minds of very many parents and preceptors a most influential if not prominent place as an object worthy of ardent desire and most painstaking exertion.

The possession of vainglory, whether distinction is to be achieved through the accrual of wealth or the attainment of position and power, is naturally an avowed object of the *world's* ambition.

It is also too frequently, in degree at least, a most important though subordinate object with the professing Christian, and the evil and mischief are in his case superadded that in this conformity to the world opportunity is afforded, it might almost be said created, and strong temptation presented for the employment of agencies in themselves essentially and positively sinful, and in seeking a forbidden end he is betrayed into the use of unhallowed and forbidden means.

So he will be whenever he has recourse to the rousing and stimulating influences of envy, covetousness, and pride.

As a consequence he will find that competition,

the usual and most popular, because commonly received as most efficacious, of methods for inducing to the putting forth of those exertions which, from whatever cause called into play, are as a general rule the indispensable conditions of the attainment of any meed of advancement, credit, or reward, in youth, or of position, influence, or fame, in subsequent years, is, as generally applied in the instruction and training of childhood and youth, a most dangerous, if not altogether objectionable, mode of endeavouring to ensure the reception of knowledge and the development of power.

The teachings and discipline of early life are at least frequently, if not in truth most generally, directed to the present or prospective gratification of family or individual pride.

Of course, both teachings and discipline are in the majority of cases also the necessary preliminaries to, and befitments for those subsequent labours by which provision is to be made for satisfying the requirements of existence, in supplying the necessities and comforts of the present life.

But even to this, the legitimate employment of necessary means, there is imparted a fearful influence for future evil, over and above the incitement to much immediate sin, through the introduction of and familiarizing with that fierce struggle for preeminence and thirst after distinction which, having the gratification of pride or of covetousness as an end, sanctions and introduces the strife of hateful and guilty passions as the recognized mean.

That competition in one sense is a necessary consequence of contemporaneous existence, under the present conditions of human life, is indisputable.

Without any intention of introducing competition, it must practically result from the force of circumstances.

But it is not to that kind of competition that we are here referring.

Ample as may be the scope afforded for the employment of false pretence, deception, and misrepresentation, in the course of that competition for employment or position which is necessarily created by the operation of the great normal principle of supply and demand, it is with the mischievous, because sinful, errors so commonly committed in the conduct of that training usually the preliminary qualification for entering upon any such competition that we would deal.

Nor could indeed any valid objection be taken to the employment of competition in examination as a test of fitness or gauge of comparative eligibility for employment.

Conducted in fairness, knowledge, and judgment, such a use of competition is in itself not only justifiable but may even seem demanded by the requirements of the gospel as to a life of consistent service to God, and for God to man.

Every class of unforbidden employment is under the gospel economy susceptible of consecration as very worship, and the admonition 'diligent in business' alone would seem to call by implication for the employment in every instance of the most suitable of agents, and efficacious of agencies, and there can be as a general rule no better method of selection on the ground of fitness than by competitive examinations as to proficiency in knowledge, ability in parts, and general fitness. The dangers, incident to the employment of competition as the great factor in the upbringing of the young, are the results of invoking as agents for rousing and stimulating to the energetic employment of the opportunities of the class-room those vicious aids of love of pre-eminence, covetousness, envy, jealousy, malevolence, and hate, the offspring of self-seeking pride, and unsanctified ambition.

These, however efficacious as incentives to personal exertion, are manifestly, however euphemistically they may be referred to as disguised blessings, or lauded as practical benefits, nevertheless real sins.

A stimulus to exertion is in the vast majority of cases an absolute necessity, but it is to be supplied in accordance with the doctrine and teaching of the gospel, not by the developing, fostering, and inculcating a desire to distance others in the race of life for the gratification of pride, or the thirst for vainglory, or any other worship of mammon, but from the hallowing and life-inspiring influence of faith in the Crucified.

Such faith, manifested in a grateful love to Jesus, will supply amplest and strongest inducement to the fullest and most zealous employment of every energy and ability, in the steady discharge of prescribed duty.

In so doing it will be all the while employing, and that with the sanction and under the benediction of heaven, those very same identical means of assiduous study and zealous application, which, in accordance with the laws of Divine providence (will of Jehovah), are in natural course generally followed by comparative, if not always conspicuously remarkable, possession of wealth, position, and power.

The believing child will thus be constrained in the course of the loving discharge of duty into the sanctified and approved attainment of that very temporal position, and material prosperity, which is the recognized and avowed goal of that race which others run, under the incitement and stimulus of unhallowed lust, envy, pride, and vain unsanctified ambition.

By such a walk of loving obedience, by such a race of faith and patience, by such contented hopeful continuance in well-doing, does that course of upbringing lead, which, starting from the recognition and acceptance of free and complete justification as the essential and absolutely necessary love-inspiring preliminary to the labours of sanctification, seeks in the steady prosecution of the latter, in entire dependence for all needed grace and strength upon the presence and power of the Holy Spirit, inspiration and motive no less than direction and government in the minutest details of conduct, not only in mature life, but also through those years of childhood and youth which afford the training time for the duties and responsibilities of after years.

CHAPTER XIII.

ADVANTAGES.

THE benefits which must accrue from the successful adoption of that system of upbringing of the young which seeks first the kingdom of heaven and its righteousness, and these moreover in that way which is strictly in accordance with the teachings of Holy Writ, will of course embrace, or at least provide for, the lawful pursuance of every object worthy an immortal being, such in every respect as man, placed for the time amid the circumstances of earthly existence.

To enumerate all the advantages absolutely involved, or thereby rendered possible of enjoyment, would be needless if possible, but there are two or three to which it may be neither out of place or unprofitable to allude.

Much disappointment, grief, vexation, and it may ofttimes be unadvisable, inconsistent, and mischievous feeling, if not display of bitterness, on the part of those who have, whether as parents or preceptors, had the charge of the young, is just the fair and reasonable result of their own errors and the natural outcome of their own faults.

For those who, in their own personal experience, have learned that even for the regenerate, endowed with and relying upon superhuman aid, the hearty desire to walk in the way of God's commandments is not by any means easy of fulfilment, and that the life of the believer is truly a condition implying unceasing watchfulness over the uprising of unexpelled evil, as well as perpetual resistance to external temptation, whilst ever and anon there is some fearful struggle to be maintained against the combined and simultaneous assault from without as well as from within, it seems in the highest degree unreasonable, and inconsistent, to look for such conduct from a poor helpless worm, endeavouring in its own unaided strength to do battle for the right and the true.

If the immolation of self, and the restraint of inborn passion, and the subjection of natural desire, is each at times too much for the man who, in the assurance of pardon for the past, and in reliance for justification entirely on the righteousness of another, and strengthened by the certainty of the promised succour of heavenly aid in the hour of danger and need, pursues the heavenward path, with what reason can these be expected of one who, without any such assistance in the time of dire extremity, is called to do battle against all the assaults of external temptation and of innate corruption ?

And yet this is just the very position in which the child is placed, who, without previous *explanation* of the absolute necessity for justification, and *acquaintance* with the sole means of obtaining it, is taught and expected to fulfil the requirements, and discharge the obligations, of the life of the sanctified.

To look for a willing, because loving, submission to the enactments of the moral law, such obedience in short as can only spring from a living faith in the Redeemer, previous to knowledge and acceptance of the gospel salvation, is to expect what is, under such circumstances, not only utterly impossible but absolutely unreasonable.

The natural heart is altogether incapable of any such emotion. And yet not a little of the religious training of the young, by the absolute, or at least virtual, prominence which is accorded, especially perhaps in very early years, to the inculcation of exemplary behaviour and moral rectitude rather than to the explanation of the gospel remedy, only by the acceptance of which can that change of disposition be obtained which is the condition essential to the obedience of love, would almost seem to reject the doctrines of innate depravity and natural impotency for good.

To treat blindness as a crime, whilst neglecting or refusing to employ its remedy, known to ourselves but not to the poor sufferer, would seem equally reasonable and just.

It may seem invidious, if not cruel, to appear to somewhat harshly animadvert upon the well-intentioned, though misdirected, zeal, which, having secured by observance of the solemn rite and sacrament of baptism a place for the infant in the visible Church, and an ostensible interest in the covenant of grace, proceeds, in the interval between then and the subsequent profession by the child of personal reliance upon the gospel

O

salvation, to virtually place it under the covenant of works.

And yet what other tendency has that prominence not unfrequently allotted in the instruction and training of the child to the keeping of the ten commandments, and other precepts of duty and charity, apart from an unmistakeably avowed and clearly explained connection with the cross of Christ.

The child is morally certain, in all the darkness of an unenlightened understanding and untutored conscience, to regard such obedience as intended *in itself* to avert *on its own account* the displeasure and secure the favour of The Heavenly Father.

Of course the child is made acquainted with Scripture history and the lives of its faithful worthies, and it may be is especially familiarized with the narrative of the earthly career of our blessed Lord and Saviour, whose life of obedience, truthfulness, gentleness, kindness, and utter self-abnegation, he is taught that he should strive to imitate, but no attempt is perhaps ever made to give *a lucid and comprehensible explanation of His work* in human guise as a Substitute, as well as an Example.

Much is heard of God's hatred of sin, but less, it may even be comparatively little, of His love to the sinner.

In short, though it is known and felt that the child can and must, if saved at all, be saved through the knowledge of the gospel, and hoped, perhaps fervently trusted, that he shall be so saved, it is considered as meantime premature or unwise to unfold, and explain, its provisions to him.

Now the result of all this is that the outward conformity of conduct to divers particulars of the requirements of the will of God is, so far as it may be exhibited, unnatural, forced, and artificial, and that the pleasing semblance of moral beauty in the child is a hollow and precarious sham.

Partly from a wish to please his parents, whom he fondly and instinctively loves, and partly from a fear of displeasing God, whom he naturally dreads, a life of more or less arduously fulfilled attention to the external requirements of morality, and the demands of religious formalism, bedecked moreover it may be, either as the outcome of constitutional tendency, or the result of parental example or surrounding influences, by much that is kindly, pleasing, generous, and lovable, is led for some time with more or less of exertion and difficulty.

So things go on till the time arrives for quitting the paternal roof, it may be in pursuit of learning, it may be for some more immediate preparation for the struggle of earning his daily bread.

Now an opportunity is afforded for lucidly explaining the way of salvation, and should it be seized, despite the inadvertencies and neglect of the past, the boy may at least enter upon this new stage of existence the joyous possessor of a true and reasonable knowledge of the truth as it is in Jesus.

But perhaps, and very probably, the sincere and hearty prayer may be unaccompanied by the words of loving explanation, and beyond general admonitions, and vague though good as affectionate advice, and perhaps the extracting of some promise to read God's Word or bend the knee in daily prayer, the poor little fellow is sent forth into the arena of school life, as ignorant of the real nature, and demands, and saving knowledge of the gospel of grace as the most benighted of distant heathen.

Possibly the religious instruction and nurture at school, which had been intended and relied on by the parents to fully supply or supplement any conscious previous deficiency on their own part, whether arising from felt or conceived personal inability or, in their opinion, lack of suitable opportunity of imparting that knowledge which they knew and felt to be, sooner or later, indispensable, proves after all little if anything superior as a mean to salvation to what had preceded.

It may be found, and perhaps not unfrequently, that (even in a school professedly conducted on Christian principles) the spiritual training may after all be described most accurately as very religious rather than truly evangelical, and the instruction in matters of doctrine so superficial and vague, and the attempts, if indeed there are any, to render it directly beneficial to the individual, so void of hearty and earnest and rational application to the necessities of his special case, that, whilst the fond parents are consoling themselves with the idea that now, when the appropriate season *has* arrived, the work of training the heart in the truth of the gospel, as well as of storing the mind with needed secular learning, is being conscientiously, zealously, and thoroughly carried on, the child is, to say the least, for all immediate purposes and practical results no better off than whilst at home.

But, assuming that, what with dread of the unseen and terror of future punishment, natural and instinctive affection for parents, jealous and watchful endeavours to preserve from the contagion of openly evil surroundings, the strong repressive measures of physical coercion, and it may be no small amount of pampering, wheedling bribery and false encouragement, childhood and boyhood have been preserved in a state of ostensible though unreal rectitude and purity, and a species of consciously most unstable moral equilibrium has been so long successfully maintained, what is to be expected when external restraints are removed and adolescence becomes youth?

In the majority of cases, then comes exposure to the full force and fury of all those manifold and terrible dangers attendant on sudden possession of freedom by those all unprepared for emancipation.

At that period of life, ere discretion has been purchased by bitter experience, and whilst as yet the proffered considerations of far-sighted prudence are not generally expected to have any great influence upon the conduct, there arise exigencies when the loudest appeals of soundest earth-born wisdom may well prove unavailing to silence the siren pleadings of awakened desire.

To successfully resist the allurements and assaults of sensual temptation, appealing as they do to the sympathy of debased natural instinct, and enlisting on their side, as they well can do, the alluring fascinations of independence and adventure, and gilding the bondage of sin with a lustre of poetry and romance, that dazzles, bewilders, and enthralls, requires far more potent aid than any to be derived from the human or the earthly, be it even from the claims of known duty or the ties of natural affection.

Even the joyous and engaging, whilst in themselves innocent, sports and recreations of youth are but poor competitors for favour when once the pruriency of imagination, hitherto restrained by the force of circumstances, has broken out into open realization of the overpowering pleasures of sensual gratification. Or even, if the invigorating sport should still hold place, it may seem manly and becoming to invest it with surroundings the very opposite of salutary and virtuous, and from an aid to virtue it may ere long degenerate into a pander to vice.

Deprived now of all the adventitious aids to virtue which had been furnished by the surroundings of home life and school discipline, the youth has been called upon to engage in a strife for which no adequate preparation had in truth been made, and as a natural consequence he falls.

And yet he does not fall at once.

The religious and, so called, moral training, such as it has been, which he has enjoyed, although unfit to avert is not altogether useless to delay.

That knowledge which has been insufficient to give pardon and peace, and with their possession to insure strength and security in the aids of heavenly power, is still ample, in the effects of an uneasy conscience, to render, at least, the first steps in open iniquity neither absolutely firm or altogether pleasant.

The bulwark of habit, so strong a defence if maintained intact, may for a time suffice, in degree at least, to stem the torrent of evil, though doomed by and by to yield before the steady pressure which hourly weakens the continuity of its encircling line. Then too, there is the never altogether quite extinguished love for the absent ones, who, though disobeyed and slighted, are still after all very dear.

At least in the lucid intervals of the blind frenzy of passion and giddy whirl of unlawful delights, there is at times it may be a yearning desire to stop for the sake of those loved ones, and there is a fearful and perpetual anxiety to lull their suspicions, and still their dreaded uneasiness, which demands a course of systematic hypocrisy from regard to them and respect to their feelings.

And then, above all, strange but fearfully possible anomaly, there may have been all along a dread of heaven's conscious displeasure that goaded to a weary and unsatisfactory struggle, intermittent but real, after self-liberation and self-justification. There may have been too, as a natural consequence of this, an irregular and blindly superstitious observance of some of the external formalities and æsthetic requirements of the religious life.

Probably, however, the manifestly unsuccessful and distasteful struggle will not be of very protracted duration, and in the reckless indifference of despair, or perhaps more likely still in the procrastination of ungrounded and delusive hopes, the child of so many prayers and expectations, pitied, lamented, but blamed all the same for failure (in a strife for which those who pity, lament, and blame had themselves in the season of opportunity done but little to prepare him), drifts helplessly on, perhaps to add to the vices of youth the sins of manhood, and to those the iniquities of old age, possibly to be for ever lost.

He had no strength by nature, and he lacked the salving omnipotence of grace, and so what wonder?

We may pretty safely assume that as a general rule the minds of those who have been brought up in religious households have been early impressed with the necessity for reconciliation with the Maker and Judge of all in order to salvation.

It may be also as reasonably taken for granted that there is moreover a settled conviction that such reconciliation is to be the result of obedience to His will.

Now, unless duly instructed as to the precise direction which such obedience is required to take under the economy of grace, the natural and it seems inevitable result of the combined effect of these two considerations (whenever a sense of imminent personal danger or the voice of conscience prompts to serious thoughts) is, to induce to efforts after working out that very self-righteousness the desire and striving after which, still as in apostolic days, together form the one grand obstacle to justification in the sight of God.

(That justification which, be it borne in mind, must ever precede sanctification of life.)

Whether such attempts are made in childhood or in early youth, although in either case more likely to prove successful in winning a temporary apparent, or even to some extent actual, victory over besetting sin than when deferred to a later period of life, they are of course worthless to satisfy the requirements of Divine justice, and, whilst liable at any moment to utterly fail, the imperfect knowledge to which they are in part at least attributable involves another class of danger.

Such danger is that to be apprehended as naturally resulting from the disheartening effects of oft-recurring failure and defeat.

It is indeed to such imperfect knowledge of the truth of the gospel as induces, or rather compels, the distressed soul to the attempting of the impossible that so many of those disappointing, grievous, and deplorable failures in the cases of really sincere seekers after salvation, reared amidst what are supposed to have been so many exceptional spiritual advantages, appear most readily attributable.

They cannot avail themselves of means with which they are unacquainted, and, as no means save those of which they are thus ignorant are really efficacious, the employment of such other as may and do most naturally suggest themselves necessarily involves failure. Repeated failure leads to disappointment. Frequent disappointment discourages. Successive discouragements disgust, deaden hope, and paralyze energy. Weariness dejects. Sorrow enervates. Strength fails. Pleasures invite. Appetite craves. Temptations allure. Sophisms deceive. Evil counsels prevail. Resistance is over, and the poor wretch is led captive by Satan at his will.

Now here is failure immediately attributable to disappointment, whilst that is equally readily accountable for on the score of sheer absolute ignorance.

Had the earliest training of such an one, although unsuccessful at the time in leading to the Saviour, had the effect of opening to the understanding and of indelibly impressing upon the mind the true *rationale* of the gospel salvation, whenever the subsequent hour of fear, terror, and anxiety had arrived, whether in schoolboy days or later, the question would have been resolved into one of acceptance or rejection of God's mercy as it really is, and is offered in the gospel of peace, and not as it is wrongly supposed and falsely pictured to be by the natural and fleshly mind.

Attempting an impossibility he naturally failed.

But he attempted the impossibility of saving himself because he had never been taught that as he never *could* so he never *need* endeavour to purchase eternal life, for it is the gift of God in Christ Jesus our Lord.

It is sad to think moreover of the amount of suffering, none the less terribly real because full oft borne in mutest sorrow, that may be entailed upon the life of such an one, even subsequent to reception of the truth.

It may be long ere he enjoys that perfect practical submission to and acquiescence in the will and pleasure of God, which, acknowledging His wisdom, and recognizing designed subserviency to His honour and glory, even in the temporary and permitted triumph of evil, can look back upon those sins of bygone years, which he knows to be pardoned, or can even endure such meed of their bitter consequences as may be in accordance with his heavenly Father's will, with a godly sorrow that harbours nought of bitterness against any save himself.

It is indeed distressing and saddening (how distressing and saddening none can adequately conceive but such as have realized in their own bitter experiences), when once the sweets and pleasures of the life of faith and love have been in any measure tasted, to feel how much of real happiness has been missed, and how much opportunity for true usefulness has been lost, through those weary years of desultory, misdirected, and all uncalled-for toil.

But when to this dreary retrospect is added the deliberately acquired conviction, that in the absence, amid all the pretentious exercises of a professedly and vauntedly religious training, of a clear exposition of the truth of the gospel is to be found the real reason for, and ready explanation of, those failures and defeats, there is a bitterness added to the cup of sorrow which, though it may not justify the expression of, can well account for the presence of an almost righteous indignation.

There is indeed another class of case wherein, unlike that just cited, the service of self and Satan has been restrained within the bounds of a respectable and decorous worldliness, and diligent study together with exemplary behaviour have ushered upon a course of life which though highly esteemed in the eyes of men is totally abhorrent in the sight of God, and one perhaps too immensely more dangerous in its influences than one of pronounced wickedness, because so much more conducive and favourable to that spiritual pride which freedom from open and indefensible profligacy is but too apt to beget and foster.

When the delusive tranquillity and self-righteous satisfaction of such a career have been suddenly disturbed by the awful realization of danger, and the true Light shines down upon life's path, perhaps well-nigh its end, how bitter the reflection that it was through ignorance of the easy entrance upon the strait and narrow way that the choice, now so manifestly wrong and so deeply deplored, had long ago been made!

In each of these cases it has been assumed that, despite the culpable inadequacy of early instruction, saving knowledge has come ere yet too late, but it may not, nor need, be always so!

Now the advantages of a clear exposition of the gospel, with the intent of, at least, firmly and indelibly impressing upon the mind of the child, as soon as may be, as the basis of all acceptable worship and true religion, a just and full knowledge of the absolute necessity for and of the perfect freeness of justification on account of Christ's finished work, and of the impossibility of pleasing God, unless first reconciled through and then living in continual dependence on the atonement of His Son as the medium of every blessing, may be either of the following.

If, as they may well be, such endeavours should be crowned with immediate success in leading the child to the Saviour, the course and work of sanctification with all its attendant benefits, spiritual, mental, and corporeal may at once be fairly entered upon.

Should the effects of such efforts be delayed till a subsequent period of life, although the work of sanctification must also, as entirely dependent thereon, be necessarily deferred, yet that clear knowledge of the mode in which salvation is to be sought and attained is so firmly implanted in the mind that the good seed may be justly regarded as there ready sown, awaiting but the vivifying influence of the Spirit of all grace.

In either event that course has been followed, dictated by inspiration, demanded by reason, directed by judgment, and approved by experience, strictest attention to which is after all but the necessary and proper use of those authorized means to ensure the child's possession of that knowledge which is essential to salvation, and the thorough and efficient employment of which is suggested by affection no less than demanded by duty, and called for by the dictates of a conscience that would fain be void of offence toward God and toward man.

It seems not only outrageous and absurd but cruel and unjust for those, who professing to hold the key of knowledge yet failed to use it aright, to blame, reproach, and disown for sins and transgressions to which they themselves have, indirectly it may be but yet actually, contributed in no small degree by their own faults and shortcomings.

CHAPTER XIV.

GETTING ON.

BESIDES those advantages just pointed out there are other, it may be less conspicuous but still most material, which result from giving to justification and sanctification each its proper place in Christian upbringing.

As well as those perils to which the Church is exposed from the widespread and increasing prevalence of false doctrine with regard to fundamental truths, there are other dangers, less heeded but by no means less real, traceable to the assimilation of sentiment and practice on the part of many of her members to those of the world without.

Admonitions against conformity to the world, if necessary in apostolic days when the line of demarcation had been so recently and firmly drawn, and when the early disciples of the cross in all the ardour and devotion of newborn faith, like a warrior colony in a hostile land, kept jealous watch and ward over truth of doctrine and purity of practice, are surely no less indispensable in this nineteenth century.

How much soever the intercourse, through so many succeeding generations, of the Church with the world has been productive of benefit to the latter, there has been all along a co-existent influence, or at least more or less effective potentiality, for evil to the Church.

The very adoption by the world of the decent and seemly externals of gospel morality has ofttimes perhaps favoured, rather than hindered, the influence and manifestation of the tendency in question, if in no other way possibly by the inducing, as it may have, the belief in a latent harmony in other respects which did not, as in truth it could not, exist.

Whatever line of ethical policy tends to suggest, much rather seems to approve or even recommend, the appropriation and adoption of the salient characteristics of the gospel morality, apart from the recognition of the absolute necessity for the gospel atonement, is dangerous in the extreme.

Even the distant approach to such a course of procedure which is to be noticed, and is in fact avowed, in many of those missionary efforts which whilst they cannot very well profess and employ respectability as a temporary religious expedient virtually would almost seem to, when seeking, if not insisting on, the attainment to a certain degree of moral elevation and decency of life as a very advisable, if not absolutely necessary, preliminary to the beneficial reception of the truth, seems of most questionable propriety, and appears, to say the least, very difficult to reconcile with the freeness as well as the avowed object of the gospel, namely, the salvation of sinners *as* sinners.

The obsequious deference paid by the world, in the acceptance of a standard of public respectability framed upon a portion of the ethics of Christianity, has obtained the all more ready ear for the misleading, and all the more dangerous because unrecognized sophistries, of artfully disguised evil counsel.

In no respect has the contaminating effect of habitual intercourse been more prominently exemplified than in regard to the apparent estimation of the comparative value, benefit, importance, and desirability of temporal advancement, material prosperity, and whatever else may be comprehended in the familiar expression, success in life.

Admitting that with some the desire of attaining wealth, position, and power may be the genuine outcome of a sincere desire by their possession to be enabled more effectually to aid the gospel cause, there seems hardly ground for any reasonable doubt but that many, possibly the vast majority of, professing Christians in the wish and endeavour to raise themselves and their families in the social scale are influenced, in the main, by motives as fleshly in their origin and as mundane in their object, as are any who engage in a similar struggle without any professed subjection to, or regard for the religion of the cross.

Yet, after all, this desire of getting on unless when *purposely* and *intentionally* made subservient, and duly subordinated, to the service, honour, and glory of the Redeemer and the advancement of His kingdom, is nothing but pure selfishness, love of the world, and desire of vainglory.

All glory is vain that is not, directly or indirectly, connected with the cross of Christ.

The desire of personal distinction, unless consecrated to the glory of Christ, is just another name for the love of vainglory.

Nor does it mend matters that this ardent striving after temporal aggrandizement, social elevation, or the distinctions of fame, may be sought to be excused or defended on the plea of a *co-existent* regard to the glory of God, but as a distinct and independent end of life. Unless intentionally and studiously sought to be made altogether absolutely designedly subservient to the glory of God, all such endeavours are apparently but futile attempts to serve God and mammon.

Nor is the liability to this specious and most dangerous delusion restricted to any special class, for in the case of each individual member of the commonwealth the question of personal advancement or family aggrandizement is after all but one of degree.

Unsanctified ambition may well enough prove the bane of existence as well for the lowliest as for the more elevated of conditions in life.

No security is afforded against the operations of this special form of lust by nature of occupation or responsibilities of office.

Even the sacred functions of the ministry to the

saints, in themselves, present no effective barrier to the ardent desire of personal advancement, and the seemly though unostentatious garb of modern puritanism or the elaborate insignia of a more ornate ritual may cover and cloak, fully as well as the robes of the lawyer, or the accoutrements of the warrior, an active and ruling spirit of self-seeking, and a restless love of pre-eminence.

Doubtless the desire of getting on has frequently, in degree at least, from time to time asserted, and that successfully, a longer or shorter temporary supremacy in the hearts and conducts of even the most consistent of men, but it should seem as if from a confluence of inviting, favouring, and auspicious circumstances, notably the opening up of so many fresh avenues to wealth, position, and distinction, the temptations to a ready submission to the sway of its influence are nowadays, more than ever, fearfully subtile and alarmingly efficacious.

Without pausing to advert at length to the causes which may have been principally and ostensibly instrumental in contributing to the existence and establishment of such a condition of affairs, it would seem most blameworthy to neglect the opportunity here afforded of alluding to that pernicious literature of a pseudo-philanthropy which, whilst extolling the exercise of the materially remunerative virtues of perseverance, sobriety, and thrift, goes so far to foster, if it does not absolutely inculcate, a spirit of self-reliance and confidence in the arm of flesh, which would virtually seem to ignore the interference of the Deity in the affairs of earth.

The very expressions so frequently on the lips of many (whose profession of faith should seem to debar from the employment of any so misleading phraseology), 'A self-made man,' 'self-help,' and suchlike idolizations of the creature, contain within them a latent potency for evil which is, alas! too little considered.

It is true, no doubt, that of those who use them, not a few do so, originally at least, with a mental reservation, tacit indeed but real, of the absolute subjection of the most painstaking and earnest and laudable and fittest of endeavours to the predeterminate will of the Most High.

Still however the habitual neglect to give open expression to such sentiments of saving qualification, restricts the beneficial effects of their influence to the breasts wherein they lie restrained and mute.

The reflex influence of language on morality, however little thought of, is a real and powerful factor whether for good or evil, and it were well indeed, if only in the interest of others (especially of the young), if the principle laid down in the Epistle of St. James, with reference to the unguarded and irreverent expression of purposes for the future, were more widely applied in the spirit of its counsel to one and all of the affairs of life.

Neglect to avow a principle of action may, much more effectually and rapidly than is frequently supposed, lead to forgetfulness of its reality and importance, and the habit of ignoring, in our conversation, the direct, and omnipotent, operation of an all-overruling providence may, ere long, lead to the contracting of habits of most decided and manifest unbelief in the exercise of its influence.

But to revert. The unsanctified desire of 'getting on,' fruitful as it is of untold present mischief and sorrow, and fraught with so much future danger and trouble as well to the state as for the individual, may nowadays, be neither inaptly or untruly characterized as the snare of the age.

Social revolutions together with political changes, subverting the bulwarks of prescriptive exclusiveness, and breaking down the barriers of hereditary advantages, have opened up to an extent unprecedented in modern times a comparatively easy access to positions of emolument, distinction, and power.

And concurrently with these changes there have been such increased facilities of locomotion, such surprises of mechanical invention, such progress in manufacturing skill, and such widely spread dissemination and popularization of information on a multitude of topics, as have largely contributed to, if they have not almost created, a general craving after change and variety, whilst at the same time they have contributed to render attainable by the many the enjoyment of pleasures, refinements, and luxuries, long necessarily restricted to the few.

Thus it has come to pass that, whilst increased facilities have been afforded for personal advancement and aggrandizement, additional inducements have been supplied for desiring their attainment.

A condition of things, it must at the same time be admitted, has been brought about, many of the advantages of which, if clearly discerned and fairly appreciated in the light of the gospel, and justly utilized in the exercise of a fervent and love-adorned faith, might well contribute in no small degree to the comfort and benefit of all classes of the community.

It is not indeed, after all, that the desire of prosperity is in itself wrong, or that its lawful enjoyment is to be spurned or deprecated.

Prosperity has undoubtedly its divinely-recognized efficiency, because its appointed office in life.

It should even seem impious to vilify or despise what God has approved.

That prosperity which, in the economy of providence, is the reward for past and accepted service (the power to perform which, by the bye, be it ever borne in mind, is never present save as the gracious gift of our heavenly Father) and the encouragement to further exertion in the discharge of duty and realization of privilege, is indeed a joy to the Almighty, for 'the Lord rejoiceth in the prosperity of His servant.'

It cannot then be itself intrinsically an evil, however through flagrant misuse it may be subservient to or productive of evil.

So too it is not in the voluntary and needless despising of prosperity but in its consistent consecration that the homage of a living faith may best be paid.

Of course exigencies may arise when to enjoy a material prosperity may be to forfeit a spiritual, and when the sacrifice of joys in themselves lawful is the unavoidable accompaniment or measure of a consistent service.

Such contingencies are, however, in the experience of the vast majority of mankind, now at least, probably of but comparatively rare occurrence.

For the modern professing Christian, as a general rule, the call is not to abjure but simply to use temporal prosperity, ' as not abusing it.'

It is abused, however, and that most frequently and most grossly.

It is abused by being regarded virtually as an absolute end and object of life, subordinate indeed in theory, but most prominent in practice.

Nor does, or indeed very well can, the evil stop here.

Acceptance of a worldly standard of importance most naturally and easily prepares the way for, and seductively allures to, the adoption of a thoroughly worldly system of tactics and procedure.

Hence most readily, if not inevitably, follows that early invocation of all those improper incentives to exertion which are derived from the considerations of pride, envy, covetousness, and real spiritual idolatry.

The forces of unhallowed emulation, inciting, goading, and compelling to a strife of jealous and hateful competition, are aroused.

The ardent desire of distinction in the school is sedulously fostered, applauded, and enjoined, not so much with a view to the attainment of efficiency for the duties of after life as from a desire of present gratification of vanity, and subsequent possession of wealth, position, and vainglory.

Sloth is denounced and punished, not so much because it is displeasing in the sight of Jesus as that it is discreditable in the eyes of men, but, above all, because it is utterly opposed to the likelihood of getting on.

Of course meanwhile the religion of the cross is professedly held in high esteem, and most reverently as well as sincerely acknowledged to be the sole foundation of every true hope for time as for eternity.

But inconsistency of belief, such as has just been portrayed, must in the natural course of events lead to untoward results.

Just as the emblem of salvation, high in air upon some cathedral dome, may be lost to sight amid the wreathing vapours of a great metropolis, so the true cross, with all its life-giving and life-consecrating influences, may soon be obscured by the clouds of incense perpetually rising from the thousand shrines of a purely selfish, and thoroughly carnal, ambition.

Assuming of course, as we well may, that the lawful enjoyment of any of the various results of getting on is in itself quite consistent with the loving service of our Lord and Saviour, nay further is in accordance with the purposes of His pleasure and decrees of His providence, the natural and fairly to be anticipated result of conscientious discharge of duty (partly perhaps as a reward and partly perhaps as an incentive), and admitting, moreover, that the attainment of material prosperity and enjoyment of the esteem or even applause of our fellows, if honestly, fairly, and justly obtained, are gratifications of lawful desires and natural instincts, wisely implanted in our breasts for the glory of God and good of the creature, it might almost seem as if in some sense the greater danger lay, not in the liability to misuse their possession, as in the tendency to seek to ensure it by wrong methods and in forbidden ways.

Of course there are evils to be anticipated from the misuse of the possession of increased temporal prosperity, but these as strictly appertaining, at least in largest measure, rather to the years of maturer life than to the period of upbringing, need not be here considered.

Now the only truly efficacious safeguard against one and all of these specious errors, which under pretence of imparting a healthful stimulus to exertion, through the employment of a self-seeking and self-glorifying competition, enthral, endanger, and destroy, is to be sought in a reasonable and consistent application of the gospel remedy as it *truly* is.

Such application conducts through the portal of complete justification, for the sake of Christ's finished substitutionary work, into that position whence, relying upon given and promised supplies of divine strength, the loving desire to do God's will in the minutest details of daily life, and, for Christ's honour and glory, to utilize every power and opportunity, supplies the best, most powerful, always safe, and ever blessed stimulus to the completest attainable success.

CHAPTER XV.

CONCLUSION.

TO some at least, if not to the majority, of those who have perused the foregoing pages it may have appeared that, however in accordance with the strict letter of gospel teaching the principles therein set forth may be, yet for a system of procedure embodying their absolute application there cannot after all be reasonably expected a very general, much less universal, adoption in practice.

It may seem, to them, as if the proposal of what should appear virtually equivalent to, if not absolutely identical with, an almost universal, or at least very general, revolution in the most commonly accepted systems of religious training of the young, no less than the proposal to utterly repudiate and ruthlessly discard the employment of the, so almost universally recognized, incitements of competition and ambition in favour of nought but the love-produced and fostered influence of a true and living faith, operating through a heaven-gifted sense of duty, should seem rather some fantastic dream of visionary pietism than a practicable outcome of sober judgment and a 'sound mind.'

And yet such a verdict might well seem hardly very consistent on the lips of such as can but lay claim to a merely general, and abstract, acquaintance (albeit so far as it goes correct) with the known theory of the Christian religion, and should appear absolutely unbecoming on the part of those who profess an implicit belief in the gospel.

That the system pursued in the upbringing of the young should be directed to the subordination of the corporeal to the spiritual, and of the temporal to the eternal, at the earliest possible opportunity in life is manifestly in strictest accordance with the most superficial knowledge of the truth.

That such subordination should be sought to be effected in that way by which alone consistent regard can be had to the inexorable requirements of Divine justice, ample provision found for the abject moral helplessness of human nature, and the prevention, so far as may be possible, of suffering on the part of their offspring efficiently ensured, is no less in accordance with the dictates of enlightened reason, than it is in strictest compliance with the teachings of revelation.

In the application of even such cold and unimpassioned consideration to the system of the gospel salvation, regarded merely as a professed specific for certain accurately defined evils, as would be extended to the consideration of any other scientific remedy, it should seem impossible but to be led to the conclusion, that such advantages are altogether unattainable in any way save by the employment of the gospel remedy as it is actually described in the pages of Holy Writ.

But, even if reason failed to approve as understanding and appreciating the absolute necessity of such a course, it should be sufficient for the professing believer that it is commanded, if not in so many words at least by the clearest, and most peremptory, implication.

The command is to preach the gospel 'to every creature.'

The gospel is a revelation of that complete salvation which combines pardon of the guilt, absolution from the penalty, and deliverance from the power and dominion of sin.

Pardon and absolution have been rendered just and equitable, as well as possible, through Christ's having made propitiation for 'the sins of the whole world,' and having wrought out a perfect righteousness, which is 'unto all and,' by imputation, 'upon all them that believe.'

There is absolutely no need for, as there is no possibility of, either making a personal satisfaction for sin or of working out a personal righteousness as a mean to justification of life.

That deliverance from the power of sin, which is identical with the personal sanctification which is the necessary preparation and indispensable befitment for the joys and associations of heaven, is promised and duly vouchsafed, more or less rapidly as may be rendered necessary by the predetermined exigencies of the individual case, to the believer, kept alive in Christ 'by the power of God,' as a sequence to the acceptance of pardon and submission to the alone justifying righteousness of God.

CONCLUSION.

Now in all these respects the gospel is a precisely defined, absolutely interharmonious, and perfectly symmetrical systematic combination of operations.

In any scientific process, disregard of the prescribed order of component steps is at least, certainly, to detract from its efficacy, and should the following of such order be absolutely requisite to the attainment of the desired results, must simply frustrate the entire undertaking.

In like manner, neglect to assign to each step its due importance, if not entailing complete failure, will at least strongly militate against entirely satisfactory results.

Now besides that mistake, in directing the endeavours of the child after sanctification, instead of to the immediate acceptance of the free and ready justification which is the *necessary* antecedent of all good and acceptable works, which has been already alluded to as so fruitful a source of failure and disappointment in the religious training of the young, there is another error of very frequent occurrence and most direful influence.

That particular of the gospel salvation which seems to be altogether overlooked by some and virtually rejected by others, is the absolute necessity of submission to the righteousness of God as a full and complete satisfaction of all the requirements of the law for the purposes of justification.

That is, in short, the acceptance of 'Christ' as 'the end of the law for righteousness.'

The result of this is that the child, never realizing its true position as entirely under free grace, whilst taught to look to Christ for pardon, is virtually left to look to itself for righteousness.

To see how utterly repugnant this is to the truth of the gospel needs but reference to the Epistle to the Romans, where the fearful consequences of refusal to submit to the righteousness of God are set forth in no uncertain, equivocal, or ambiguous terms.

The practical results of this untrue, because inadequate, representation of the gospel remedy, bad as they are in the experience of grown-up members of the visible Church, should seem even still more disadvantageous to the best interests of humanity when developed in the case of the young.

Although not perhaps equally perilous with the error of treating sanctification as precedent to justification, because approaching nearer the true process of salvation, it has dangers peculiar to itself, not the least prominent of which is the disheartening influence which it necessarily exerts on the endeavours of the insufficiently instructed seeker after peace.

The young who have learned to look to Jesus rather as 'a helper' to salvation than as 'a complete Saviour,' seek in a diligent and painstaking attention to formal religion to please God, by living in accordance with the moral teachings of Scripture, perhaps notably of the New Testament, and above all of our blessed Lord and Saviour's personal discourses.

But all the while, in the absence of a known reconciliation with their heavenly Father, there is a sense of compulsion connected with their obedience which, though it may not always render it perhaps positively irksome, marks the inducement to such service as something very different to the pleasantly constraining influence of grateful love.

It may indeed be that, at times, they do experience a degree of conscious temporary satisfaction in the discharge of duty, or the achievement of self-sacrifice, which may even pass current for a holy joy, but which, if thoroughly analyzed, would probably be found to be rather a sense of gratification at having succeeded in so far keeping

God's commandments as to feel entitled to His favour.

They are, although in a measure sincerely depending upon the Saviour, reckoning upon His aid as conditional, to some extent at least, on their doing their very best.

They are in fact striving to work out their own salvation in regard, not to sanctification (a scripturally recognized, appointed, and approved course of labour, wherein they would be the grace-honoured co-workers with the Almighty Spirit) but to justification. By so doing they are, none the less really although it be in consequence of ignorance, whilst assuming themselves to be pleasing God, really living in unbelief, so far as practically denying the full efficacy of the sacrifice and sufferings of His only-begotten and well-beloved Son.

The result is, that though it may be long protracted, the struggle against evil becomes more and more feeble and intermittent in its nature, till at last it is given up, it might almost be said from the sheer overpowering force of dire necessity, and just from the lack of such sufficient inspiration to its faithful and patient continuance as is alone derivable from the constraining efficacy of the love of Christ,

CONCLUSION.

Love to Christ is not natural to the human breast.

Love is neither respect or admiration, or even dutiful allegiance. It is something far more than all these combined.

The presence in the heart of man of love to Christ is brought about through the knowledge of His love to us, and just in proportion to our appreciation of that love will be the measure of its potency as a motive in life.

The great means of showing forth that love is the announcement of the wonders of the Atonement.

Just then in proportion as the fulness and freeness of that mighty remedy are truly displayed, can the presence of love to Christ be alone reasonably and justly anticipated.

Of course it does not necessarily follow that the most lucid delineation and impassioned commendation of the love of Jesus are, in themselves, sufficient to awaken one spark of responsive affection.

Save as employed, empowered, and prospered by the Holy Spirit, that reason and rhetoric, which in respect to other matters might be irresistible, must, with regard to this, be of no avail.

But it is with the dutiful and reasonable employment of appointed means that we have to do, and save in the truthful setting forth of free and full salvation, as it is actually announced in the gospel, there exists no appointed means for the rescue of the soul whether of adult or of child.

The salvation for the one, as for the other, whether as regards pardon, justification, sanctification, or future glory, is all of grace.

It does not matter how near any given system may approach in general likeness, or how it may seem to identically coincide in not a few particulars, if it does not absolutely agree with 'the truth as it is in Jesus' in allotting its proper place, and due relative importance, to each proffered advantage of the great and only salvation it is not the gospel.

To look for certain results, which are attainable only through the acceptance of the gospel, from the employment of any such substituted system, is simply unwarrantable and absurd.

Now what measure of success can be justly anticipated from any course of religious instruction wherein there is a manifest failure to recognize this as true?

The law is not the gospel, however undoubtedly

the benefits derivable from its acceptance, as a rule of life, are inseparably connected with obedience to the gospel.

When the teaching of the law is virtually resorted to instead of the preaching of the gospel, to look for those effects upon the life which can only be brought about by the reception of the latter is to expect an impossibility.

Every conversion is a miracle. With the unseen operations of that almighty power by which that miracle is wrought man has nothing to do, save to place himself, or seek to bring others within their scope by obedience to the gospel.

It is in the too frequent pursuance of such a course (the teaching of the law instead of the preaching of the gospel) that a ready solution may, very probably, not at all unfrequently be found for that, to many, most perplexing of problems, the frequent, proverbial, and sometimes desperate failures and falls of the children of professedly Christian parents.

They have been brought up under the law and not under the gospel.

They have been expected and, so far as appearances go, perhaps successfully induced or compelled, to join in the employments and participate in the enjoyments becoming the life of faith, whilst as yet unconverted and absolutely carnally-minded.

Moral compulsion and physical restraint, together with the instinctive attachments of natural affection, have in combination sufficed, it may be for years, to keep up at least a propriety of demeanour which may have even induced to the hope that all was indeed well.

But such a life, with its systematic practice of hypocrisy and deceit, enforced it might even be almost said by the very apparent necessity of their employment merely that life at home should be endurable, is naturally forsaken as soon as opportunity offers, for a, should it be merely temporary, throwing off the thraldom of such hateful bondage.

Of course for them it *is* a hateful bondage, it would have been in all probability felt as such by the parents themselves prior to their own conversions.

Now if parents could only be brought to see that all such enforced show of service to God, if it be not the result of wilful substitution of the law for the gospel, is at least very like or practically amounts to a virtual placing of sanctification before justification, and as such should be regarded as not only unacceptable in God's sight but altogether inappropriate to, if not absolutely militating against, the attainment of the very desire of their hearts (the godly upbringing of their offspring), they would surely pause ere they either encouraged or compelled to its performance.

Instead of straining every effort after the maintenance of such a life as is only consistent with, as it is only possible after, a prior reconciliation, they would direct every energy to the setting forth of the gospel in all its simplicity and freeness, leaving the natural, and inevitable, results of its acceptance, in the willing obedience of a consecrated life, to follow in due course.

Nor would they at the same time fail to endeavour, by the fullest exhibition in their own behaviours of the happy and blessed fruits of faith, to entice to its exercise in the acceptance of a salvation so manifestly productive of peace, and joy, and loving-kindness.

The familiar narrative of how the single-minded Moravians, amid the ice-bound regions of the dreary North, convinced by bitter disappointment of the utter impotence of considerations of wrath and punishment to influence the stolid hearts of those whom they had come to save, and disheartened well-nigh to despair, discovered in the theme of a Saviour's dying love a power to melt the heart, and kindle hope, and fill with life, and love, and energy, the ignorant and degraded savage, is one which might well be pondered and taken to heart by full many a father and mother.

The failures they dread, or deplore, are immediately instrumentally attributable to the absence of that conversion, change of purpose and aim, which is indispensable to that life of willing gospel obedience which is the only guarantee for true success in life.

Such conversion is not to be expected, just because the appointed instrumentality for its attainment through the acceptance of the gospel, as it really is, has not been provided for by honest, full, and lucid explanation.

To justly provide for the attaining of that result which they so sincerely desire and so zealously and persistently seek to ensure, there is but one way, and that is through the personal acceptance by the objects of their solicitudes of the gospel offer.

And yet how can such believe unless they hear?

Such acceptance does not consist in, and neither

can it be compelled to by, enforced submission to the bitter and repulsive slavery, drudgery, and irksome routine of a life of seemingly cold and, to them, unmeaning religious formalism, for the observance of which unrenewed nature could hardly be expected to have either aptitude or desire.

A wearisome incessant counselling, a ceaseless harassing interference, a bondage of superfluous restriction, and perhaps a manifestly arbitrary and unjust recourse to punishment, serve but to embitter, disgust, and further alienate and estrange, and instead of favouring the reception of even such imperfect religious teachings as may be sought to be imparted have rather the tendency, or effect, of strengthening tenfold the innate aversion to *everything* spiritual.

Of course moreover all this is materially strengthened should the quick-witted child discern a manifest inconsistency, in the behaviour of those who are over it, with the principles which they so frequently announce, or which it, in any other way, may learn to be identified with the religion of which they talk so much.

To the believer of course such inconsistencies would be, though matters of regret, too easily accountable for, but to the ignorant and unbelieving they are simply stumbling-blocks and readily available excuses for wilful persistence in evil.

To discern failure as, not only explainable by, but justly and reasonably attributable to the neglect of the sole mean adequate to provide for success, or, what amounts practically to the same thing, to such an unreasonable, inconsistent, faulty, or incomplete employment of such remedy as is, temporarily at least, almost equally disadvantageous with its absolute rejection, is the first step toward the adoption of such sole adequate mean in its entirety and efficacy.

The obstinacy of inveterate custom and the force of habit, although enlisted on the side of error and perhaps all the while half-consciously self-condemned, cannot be expected to yield without a struggle, and plausible excuses will not be wanting for withholding the announcement of the glad tidings in all their freeness and fulness from childhood and early youth, until apparently sufficiently prepared for their reception by a necessary system of legal training.

Besides the assumed incapacity of comprehension, to which allusion has been already made in a prior chapter, it may be pleaded, and that with some show of reason and justice, that some means *must* be employed to crush and restrain the unruly passions and tempers of the human breast, and that the discipline of severity is not only justifiable but at times indispensable.

So it undoubtedly may be, when its exercise is fairly and justly demanded, as it undeniably may be in certain exigencies.

But if those who are but too willing and ready to accept of its admitted indispensability, under such circumstances, as a pretext for the authorized maintenance of an arbitrary despotism, and a not always absolutely righteous, however well-intentioned, coercion, as at least most fittingly preparative to the reign of grace, would follow the analogy of the Divine government, they might there find little or no precedent for such a course.

They would find that though therein punishment, as threatened, is certain, it is long deferred, nor does the rod of correction fall till after long and fruitless exercise of the most long-suffering patience and employment of the most loving and tender suasion, that judgment itself is ever tempered with mercy, and legislation framed in compassionate regard to the manifold infirmities of human nature, and that moreover in no case is sin punished without having been first unmistakeably defined either by the declarations of revelation or the monitions of conscience.

Punishment of the fruits of inevitable ignorance is wanton cruelty, and when such ignorance is fairly attributable to our own neglect to instruct, gross injustice.

The parent or preceptor who punishes, or even reproaches, for conduct, the indubitable result of his having kept back that knowledge by the possession of which it could alone be reasonably and effectually sought to be prevented, is guilty of both cruelty and injustice.

With regard to that employment of the vicious incentives of covetousness in whatever form, and more especially as applied in the strife of competition for the sole purpose of gratifying pride and satisfying a desire of self-aggrandizement, inconsistent as such must on due consideration manifestly appear, not only with the letter but the spirit of gospel teaching, it can only be fairly attributed to the influence of that spirit of worldly-mindedness which is now, as it has been from the first, the bane, snare, and curse of the domestic, social, and political life of professing Christendom.

That the mistakes attendant on the inconsistent and illogical attempts to train up the young which so generally pass current for religious instruction should be committed with the best of intentions, and in absolute integrity of mind and sincerity of motive, to say nothing of their even forming subjects for gratulation and eulogy, is perhaps to the reflective mind the most painfully distressing aspect of the question.

Much as they may be the result of unbelief, they may after all be due to no small extent to ignorance of the truth.

At least with regard to the fundamental errors of diffidence, or inadequacy, in explanation to the young of the gospel remedy it may well be that a full and free justification is not proclaimed and pre-eminently insisted on (as the indispensable condition to the commencement of a life of Christian service), just because those whose duty it is to announce the truth do not themselves sufficiently realize alike the sufficiency and indispensability of justification by faith, or acknowledge its true position and purpose in the operation of personal salvation.

Of that justification the two great component constituent parts are pardon and righteousness.

That righteousness is a complete satisfaction of all the requirements of the law, wrought out by our Lord and Saviour on behalf of every believer, and *freely* offered for acceptance.

Submission to that righteousness is the *indispensable* condition of justification.

There is absolutely no other mode of being regarded as righteous in the sight of God save by its imputation.

Neglect to fearlessly announce and insist upon the indispensability of belief, that is the acceptance and practical application, of *this* truth, is the key to much of that failure and disappointment which attaches to so much of the religious teaching of the day in pulpit, school, and family.

It is utterly vain to expect the good effects of the gospel on the character and life, save as the gospel is known and accepted.

Submission to this righteousness of God is absolutely necessary to justification, and he who keeps back the knowledge of its existence, nature, and indispensability, does not teach the gospel, however he may seek to instil other departments of scriptural knowledge, or inculcate Christian morality.

Sincerity, devotion, and weariest toil in pursuing a wrong way will not cause it to conduct to the desired goal.

The way to peace opens not amid the drear, and sterile, and awe-inspiring depths of the Sinaitic desert, but beneath the cross on Calvary.

'Them that honour me I will honour,' is the declaration of Divine truth.

For those who have heard of the great salvation it is a duty, no less than a privilege, to honour Him who achieved it by the readiest acknowledgment and heartiest acceptance of *every* benefit purchased by His labour, sufferings, and death.

There is in fact for those to whom the great salvation has been revealed no other way of acceptably honouring God.

How far too inadequately do even His own saints appreciate the truth that save on His account, and through His mediation, it is impossible for the Almighty Father of all to regard save with abhorrence, much less acknowledge, accept, and reward, any tribute, even of sincerest worship and heartiest praise, from His fallen, sinful, and degraded children !

Just in proportion as we honour Him in the accepting, proclaiming, and utilizing of Christ's great work of substitution, as being indeed, what it professes to be, an absolutely sufficient and perfect, once for ever accomplished, atonement 'for all the sins of the whole world,' and an absolute available satisfaction, for the purposes of personal justification, of every demand of the law, may we expect 'that honour which cometh of God.'

Nor need we fear lest by so doing we shall be following a course opposed, in any degree, to the best and truest regard to even our temporal interests.

The histories of nations and the records of private lives alike testify to the frequently truly marvellous, though it may be at times long deferred yet ever certainly in some way vouchsafed, fulfilment of this promise.

But, besides those motives for the clear and full enunciation of the truth of the gospel to the understanding of the child and its consistent application to the conduct of youthful upbringing already referred to, there are others which, though they may seem to some too much derived from considerations of sentiment, cannot nevertheless, on that account, be either dismissed with justice or disregarded with impunity.

If that desire to provide for the future welfare and comfort of their offspring, when they themselves are dead and gone, which directed into wrong channels is so often the unintentional cause of so much misfortune and misery, were but enlightened by a due appreciation of the poignant griefs, and perhaps temporally irremediable troubles, which mistakes in early nurture may entail in after years upon the objects of their affection, how different, for many, might be the retrospect of life to what it really proves!

When the sun is slowly sinking amid a blaze of glory in the western sky, and the gentle breezes of eventide are softly sighing 'mid the darkening shades of the surrounding woods, and the lone bearer of some heavy cross stands weary and pensive by the silent tomb, what a fearful and unutterable intensity of bitterness is added to the already well-nigh unbearable anguish of remorseful grief, the natural and inevitable consequence of years of wildest profligacy and maddest sin, to feel these after all in any degree indubitably referable to and inseparably linked with the errors and neglects, albeit of ignorance and misdirected zeal, of those the loving memory of whom is nevertheless cherished in the deepest recesses of his rent and weary heart!

Well does the writer remember reading a most truly affecting narrative of the sad end of a poor prodigal, dying in a distant clime.

In it full much was made of the touching episode of an unopened and long neglected letter.

It contained the announcement of all having been done necessary for his restoration to his deserted home.

The ship had been ready to bear him back, but he knew it not.

The news came long years too late.

But there was a depth of pathos added to the otherwise sufficiently saddening tale by the revelations of early life incidental to that letter.

It seemed as if this display of, all undreamt of, solicitude had been the direct outcome of the reception of such views of the Saviour's forgiving love as had completely melted a parent's heart.

It left the impression that had that love borne earlier equal sway in that home, in all its fulness and subduing efficacy, the wanderer had, in all probability, never departed, and, instead of the anguish of a well-nigh hopeless end, he had yielded his spirit in the 'sure and certain' hope of a glorious resurrection.

The writer cannot but think, as it has long appeared to him, that the failures and profligacy of the children of professing Christians are, far more frequently than is generally recognized and acknowledged, intimately connected with, if not immediately traceable to, the unbelief of those who brought them up.

Such unbelief may be manifested in a variety of details, but is all readily inclusive under the heads of omission to sufficiently early and lucidly *explain* the Gospel in its fulness, freeness, and truth, and of inconsistency with the requirements of its morality in the methods of their training and management of the Child.

A SELECTION FROM
James Nisbet & Co.'s Publications.

OVER THE HOLY LAND. By the Rev. J. A. WYLIE, LL.D., Author of 'The History of Protestantism.' Crown 8vo, cloth, 7s. 6d.

CHARACTERISTICS OF CHRISTIANITY. By the Rev. Professor STANLEY LEATHES, D.D. Professor of Hebrew, King's College, London. Crown 8vo, 6s.

INFORMATION AND ILLUSTRATIONS FOR PREACHERS AND TEACHERS. By the Rev. G. S. BOWES, Author of 'Illustrative Scripture Gatherings.' Crown 8vo, cloth, 5s.

OBSCURE CHARACTERS AND MINOR LIGHTS OF SCRIPTURE. By the Rev. FREDERICK HASTINGS. Crown 8vo, 5s.

THE HOMILETICAL LIBRARY. By the Rev. Canon SPENCE, M.A., and the Rev. J. S. EXELL, M.A. Vol. I. containing Sermons appropriate for Advent, Christmas, and New Year. Demy 8vo, 7s. 6d. Also, *just ready*, Vol. II., containing Outline Sermons suitable for Epiphany, Septuagesima, Sexagesima, and Quinquagesima. Demy 8vo, 7s. 6d. (To be completed in Eight Volumes.)

'Of all books of this character published in this country, the present must take its place in the first rank.'—*Liverpool Mercury*.

THE NATURAL ELEMENTS OF REVEALED THEOLOGY. Being the Baird Lecture for 1881. By the Rev. GEORGE MATHESON, D.D. Crown 8vo, cloth, 6s.

'Few men in the Church could write a book of such distinguished merit.'—*Homilist*.

GLIMPSES THROUGH THE VEIL; or, Some Natural Analogies and Bible Types. By JAMES WAREING BARDSLEY, M.A., Author of 'Illustrative Texts and Texts Illustrated.' Crown 8vo, cloth, 5s.

LIFE OF MRS. STEWART SANDEMAN OF BONSKEID AND SPRINGLAND. By Mrs. G. F. BARBOUR, Author of 'The Way Home.' Crown 8vo, cloth, 6s.

DAILY EVENING REST. By Miss AGNES GIBERNE, Author of 'Decima's Promise.' 16mo, cloth, 2s. 6d.

THE HOLY SUPPER. Short Chapters for Young Communicants. By the Rev. W. KENNEDY MOORE, D.D. 16mo, cloth, 1s.
'A series of letters, very scriptural and earnest.'—*Catholic Presbyterian.*

MY LORD'S MONEY. By the Rev. ERNEST BOYS, Author of 'The Sure Foundation.' 16mo, cloth, 1s.

IS ALL WELL? By CHRISTIAN REDFORD, Author of 'The Kingdom.' 16mo, 1s.

ABOUT OURSELVES. By Mrs. HENRY WOOD, Author of 'Bessie Wells.' Small crown 8vo, cloth, 1s. 6d.

THE SAVIOUR'S CALL. By the Rev. F. WHITFIELD, M.A. Small crown 8vo, cloth, 1s. 6d.

VOICE OF JESUS, DAY BY DAY. By Mrs. MACRAE. Small crown 8vo, cloth, 2s. 6d.

POPPIES AND PANSIES. By EMMA MARSHALL, Author of 'Cathedral Cities of England,' etc. Crown 8vo, cloth, Illustrated, 5s.

SIR VALENTINE'S VICTORY, and Other Stories. By EMMA MARSHALL. Crown 8vo, cloth, Illustrated, 3s. 6d.

KATHLEEN. By Miss AGNES GIBERNE. Crown 8vo, Illustrated, cloth, 5s.

MOTHER'S QUEER THINGS. By Miss ANNA WARNER, Author of 'What Aileth Thee?' etc. Crown 8vo, cloth, Illustrated, 2s. 6d.

LADY TEMPLE'S GRANDCHILDREN. By Miss EVERETT GREEN. Crown 8vo, cloth, Illustrated, 3s. 6d.

PARABLES OF JESUS. By the Rev. JAMES WELLS, Author of 'Bible Echoes,' etc. Crown 8vo, cloth, Illustrated, 5s.

CISSY'S TROUBLES. By DARLEY DALE, Author of 'Little Bricks.' Crown 8vo, cloth, Illustrated, 3s. 6d.

SPOILT GUY. By DARLEY DALE. Crown 8vo, cloth, Illustrated, 2s. 6d.

SUNDAY PARABLES. By the Rev. W. J. MATHAMS. Crown 8vo, cloth, 2s. 6d.

LIFE'S MUSIC; or, My Children and Me. By Mrs. HORNIBROOK, Author of 'Through Shadow to Sunshine,' Crown 8vo, cloth, Illustrated, 5s.

THE CHILDREN'S PILGRIMAGE. By Mrs. L. T. MEADE, Author of 'A London Baby.' Crown 8vo, cloth, Illustrated, 5s.

FOR THE WORK OF THE MINISTRY: A Manual of Homiletical and Pastoral Theology. By W. GARDEN BLAIKIE, D.D., LL.D., Professor of Apologetics, and of Ecclesiastical and Pastoral Theology, New College, Edinburgh. Crown 8vo, cloth, 5s.
'It covers a wide territory, and discusses very many questions about which it must be of great service to a young minister to know the judgment of a wise and earnest man.'—*Congregationalist.*

LONDON: JAMES NISBET & CO., 21 BERNERS STREET.

THE PUBLIC MINISTRY AND PASTORAL METHODS OF OUR LORD. By W. GARDEN BLAIKIE, D.D., LL.D., Professor of Apologetics, and of Ecclesiastical and Pastoral Theology, New College, Edinburgh. Crown 8vo, cloth, 6s.

THE ATONEMENT: A Clerical Symposium. By Various Writers. (Reprinted from the 'Homiletic Magazine.') Crown 8vo, 6s. Among the Contributors are the Bishop of Amycla, Dr. R. F. Littledale, Professor Israel Abrahams, Archdeacon Farrar, Principal Robert Rainy, Crosby Barlow, and the Rev. G. W. Olver.

MEMORIALS OF THE LATE FRANCES RIDLEY HAVERGAL. By her Sister, MARIA V. G. HAVERGAL. Crown 8vo, cloth, 6s. With Portrait and other Illustrations. Also a Cheaper Edition, crown 8vo, price 6d. sewed, cloth, 1s. 6d.

THE NEW TESTAMENT SCRIPTURES: Their Claims, their History, and their Authority. Being the Croall Lecture for 1882. By the Rev. A. H. CHARTERIS, D.D., Professor of Biblical Criticism in the University of Edinburgh. Demy 8vo, cloth, 7s. 6d.

'In these days of somewhat superficial scepticism, a book of thorough scholarship and weighty argument like this is a great boon.'—*British Quarterly.*

OUR CHRISTIAN CLASSICS. Readings from the Best Divines, with Notices, Biographical and Critical. By the late Rev. JAMES HAMILTON, D.D. Complete in Four Volumes. Crown 8vo, cloth, 16s.

THE CULTURE OF PLEASURE; or, The Enjoyment of Life in its Social and Religious Aspects. By the Author of 'The Mirage of Life.' Crown 8vo, cloth, 3s. 6d.

EXETER HALL LECTURES. Delivered before the Young Men's Christian Association from 1845-46 to 1864-65. Uniform re-issue in Twenty Volumes, handsomely bound in cloth. Price 4s. each Volume; or the complete set, £3.

STEPS THROUGH THE STREAM; or, Daily Readings for a Month. By MARGARET STEWART SIMPSON. With an Introduction by Mrs. BARBOUR, Author of 'The Way Home,' etc. 16mo, cloth, 1s.

'The sweetness of tone and beneficence of spirit will make the book a favourite with many.'—*Christian.*

WELLS OF WATER. By Mrs. SIMPSON, Author of 'Steps through the Stream,' etc. Square 16mo, cloth elegant, 1s.

'It is fitted to exercise a brightening and sweetening influence on life.'—*Daily Review.*

STORIES OF THE CATHEDRAL CITIES OF ENGLAND. By EMMA MARSHALL, Author of 'Matthew Frost,' 'Stellafont Abbey,' etc. With Illustrations. Crown 8vo, cloth, 5s.

'These "Stories" are told with great freshness and descriptive power, and will be read with interest by all.'—*Nonconformist.*

LONDON: JAMES NISBET & CO., 21 BERNERS STREET.

BIBLE CHILDREN. Studies for the Young. By the Rev. JAMES WELLS, M.A., Author of 'Bible Echoes.' Illustrated. Small crown 8vo, cloth, 3s. 6d.

'One of the wisest and best sets of addresses to children we remember to have seen.'—*Baptist.*

ARCHIBALD CAMPBELL TAIT: A Sketch of the Public Life of the late Archbishop of Canterbury. By A. C. BICKLEY. Small crown 8vo, cloth, 2s. 6d.

JOYFUL SERVICE: A Sketch of the Life and Work of Emily Streatfeild. By her SISTER. Crown 8vo, cloth, 1s.

'An exceedingly interesting record of a noble and devoted life.— *Church Bells.*

ABIDE IN CHRIST. Thoughts on the Blessed Life of Fellowship with the Son of God. Small crown 8vo, cloth, 2s. 6d.

GOD'S ANSWERS: The Narrative of Miss Annie Macpherson's Work at the Home of Industry, Spitalfields, and also in Canada. By Miss LOWE, Author of 'Punrooty.' Crown 8vo, Illustrated, cloth, 3s. 6d.

THE PRINCE IN THE MIDST. By SOPHIA M. NUGENT. With a Preface by the Rev. C. A. FOX. 16mo, cloth, 1s.

'This little book contains many beautiful meditations.'—*Christian.*

THE UPPER SPRINGS AND THE NETHER SPRINGS; or, Life Hid with Christ in God. By ANNA SHIPTON. Small crown 8vo, 2s. 6d. cloth.

'The volume is full of personal illustrations of religious devotedness, which those who are called upon to address old or young will know how to value and employ.'—*Liverpool Mercury.*

EVENING STARS. By Mrs. EVERED POOLE. 32mo, cloth, 9d. This volume is written on the plan intended to have been carried out by Miss F. R. Havergal, as described in the preface to 'Morning Stars.'

'Contains thirty-one shining promises, illuminated by stories, which children will love to read.'—*Christian.*

THE LORD'S PURSEBEARERS. By HESBA STRETTON. Crown 8vo, cloth, 1s. 6d.

'Full of power and pathos.'—*Liverpool Mercury.*

AN EXPOSITION OF THE OLD AND NEW TESTAMENTS, wherein each Chapter is summed up in its Contents; the Sacred Text inserted at large in Distinct Paragraphs, each Paragraph reduced to its Proper Heads; the Sense given, and largely Illustrated; with Practical Remarks and Observations. By MATTHEW HENRY. In Nine Volumes imperial 8vo, cloth, reduced to £2, 2s.

LONDON: JAMES NISBET & CO., 21 BERNERS STREET

WORKS BY THE LATE FRANCES RIDLEY HAVERGAL.

Small 4to, cloth gilt, 12s.,
LIFE ECHOES. With Twelve Chromo-Lithograph Illustrations, by the Baroness HELGA VON CRAMM.

Small 4to, 12s.,
SWISS LETTERS. With Twelve Illustrations, by the Baroness HELGA VON CRAMM.

Small 4to, in extra cloth gilt, 12s.,
LIFE MOSAIC: 'The Ministry of Song' and 'Under the Surface.' In One Volume. With Twelve Illustrations of Alpine Scenery and Flowers, by the Baroness HELGA VON CRAMM. Printed in colours, under the superintendence of the Artist, by KAUFMANN of Baden.

Small 4to, 12s. cloth extra,
LIFE CHORDS. Earlier and Later Poems. With Illustrations of Alpine Scenery and Flowers, by the Baroness HELGA VON CRAMM.

32mo, 1s. 6d. cloth,
THE MINISTRY OF SONG.
Crown 8vo, 5s. cloth; Cheap Edition, royal 32mo, 1s. 6d. cloth, gilt edges,
UNDER THE SURFACE.
Last Poems of the late FRANCES RIDLEY HAVERGAL.

Royal 32mo, 1s. 6d. cloth extra, gilt edges,
UNDER HIS SHADOW. With a Preface by her Sister.

Royal 32mo, 9d. cloth,
MORNING STARS; or, Names of Christ for His Little Ones.

Royal 32mo, each 6d. sewed; 9d. cloth,
MORNING BELLS AND LITTLE PILLOWS: Being Waking and Good Night Thoughts for the Little Ones.

Royal 16mo, 1s. cloth,
THE FOUR HAPPY DAYS.
Small crown 8vo, 3s. 6d. cloth; Cheap Edition, 1s. 6d. limp cloth; 1s. paper,
BRUEY, A LITTLE WORKER FOR CHRIST.

Fcap. 4to, 3s. cloth, gilt edges; or in paper cover, 1s. 6d.,
SONGS OF PEACE AND JOY. The Words selected from 'The Ministry of Song' and 'Under the Surface.' Music by CHARLES H. PURDAY.

ROYAL GRACE AND ROYAL GIFTS.
Embracing the following Seven Books in a Neat Cloth Case, with Lid, price 10s. 6d. These Books may be had separately, 16mo, price 1s. each.

KEPT FOR THE MASTER'S USE.
THE ROYAL INVITATION; or, Daily Thoughts on Coming to Christ.
LOYAL RESPONSES; or, Daily Melodies for the King's Minstrels.
MY KING; or, Daily Thoughts for the King's Children.
ROYAL COMMANDMENTS; or, Morning Thoughts for the King's Servants.
ROYAL BOUNTY; or, Evening Thoughts for the King's Guest.
STARLIGHT THROUGH THE SHADOWS.

LONDON: JAMES NISBET & CO., 21 BERNERS STREET.

WORKS BY REV. J. JACKSON WRAY.

HONEST JOHN STALLIBRASS. Illustrated, crown 8vo, cloth plain, 3s. 6d.; cloth gilt, 5s.

GARTON ROWLEY; or, Leaves from the Log of a Master Mariner. Crown 8vo, Illustrated, 3s. 6d.

LIGHT FROM THE OLD LAMP; or, Homespun Homilies for the Crowd. Crown 8vo, cloth, 5s.

A NOBLE VINE. Crown 8vo, cloth, 3s. 6d.

MATTHEW MELLOWDEW. Crown 8vo, cloth, 5s.

NESTLETON MAGNA. Crown 8vo, cloth, 3s. 6d.; cloth, gilt edges, 5s.

PETER PENGELLY. Crown 8vo, 2s.

PAUL MEGGITT'S DELUSION. Crown 8vo, cloth, 3s. 6d.

A MAN EVERY INCH OF HIM. Crown 8vo, cloth, 3s. 6d.

THE CHRONICLES OF CAPSTAN CABIN. Crown 8vo, cloth, 3s. 6d.

WORKS BY SAMUEL GILLESPIE PROUT.

NEVER SAY DIE: A Talk with Old Friends. 16mo, sewed, 6d.; cloth, 9d.

HURRAH! A Bible Talk with Soldiers. 16mo, sewed, 6d. cloth, 9d.

ALONE IN THE FIELD. 32mo, sewed, 2d.

WHOSE LUCK: A Bit of a Talk with Fishermen. 32mo sewed, 2d.

WORKS BY THE REV. ERNEST BOYS, M.A.

THE SURE FOUNDATION. 16mo, cloth, 1s.
LIFE OF CONSECRATION. 16mo, cloth, 1s.
REST UNTO YOUR SOULS. 16mo, cloth, 1s.
FILLED WITH THE SPIRIT. 16mo, cloth, 1s.
MY LORD'S MONEY. 16mo, cloth, 1s.

LONDON: JAMES NISBET & CO., 21 BERNERS STREET.

www.ingramcontent.com/pod-product-compliance
Lightning Source LLC
Chambersburg PA
CBHW031252250426
43672CB00029BA/2228